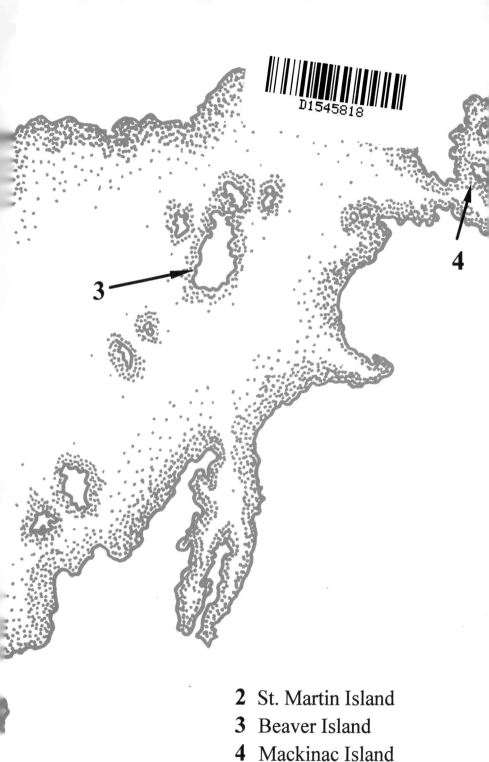

D1545818

3

4

2 St. Martin Island
3 Beaver Island
4 Mackinac Island

This edition of *Washington Island* is dedicated to the late Conan Bryant Eaton in recognition of his many contributions to Island history. As we prepared this work, we became ever more aware of his distinctive style, meticulous research and attentiveness to detail.

WASHINGTON ISLAND

1836-1876

A part of the history of Washington Township

by
Conan Bryant Eaton

Jackson Harbor Press

Copyright © 1972, 1980 by Conan Bryant Eaton
Copyright © 1997 by Town of Washington
Historical Archives Committee
All rights reserved

Published 1972
Revised edition 1980
Second printing 1987
Third edition 1997

Published by
Jackson Harbor Press
RR1, Box 107AA
Washington Island, WI 54246

Printed in USA

Publisher's Cataloging-in-Publication Data
Eaton, Conan Bryant, 1909-1991
Washington Island, 1836-1876 by Conan Bryant
    Eaton; with cover illustration by Kate West
Summary: History of Washington Island from
    1836 to 1876
                1. Door County, WI --Washington
                Island 2. Icelandic immigrants
I. West, Kate, ill.
II. Title
977.5

Library of Congress Catalog Card Number
97-71860

ISBN 0-9640210-9-9

FOREWORD

The focus of this book is upon the eventful forty year period between 1836 and 1876 when the Town of Washington was formed. This was the era when permanent settlers replaced transient visitors, when a handful of Yankee and Irish fishermen gave way to a growing migration of Scandinavians, first Norwegians and Danes, and later Icelanders and Swedes. Agriculture joined commercial fishing and lumbering as viable ways of earning a living.

This is the story of the town's beginning and of the struggles men and women faced in establishing homes in the wilderness for themselves and their families. Surrounded throughout the year by water and ice, the Island was at times a remote outpost on the fringe of civilization. And at other times, it was a busy haven for fishermen and a port-of-call for re-fueling lake vessels. Situated upon a major avenue of commerce in Lake Michigan, Islanders were often better informed of developments elsewhere than those in similar-sized communities inland.

Initially, Island life centered upon its harbors, with Washington Harbor being first settled. Residents survived on a diet of fresh and salted fish, and on home-grown potatoes and other vegetables. Homesteaders, forever short of money, built their own cabins. Few could afford costly goods brought in from elsewhere. Yet they survived and ultimately prospered.

In 1870, four bachelors from Iceland were persuaded to move to the Island from their temporary residence in Milwaukee. In their native land, trees did not grow but here trees grew everywhere. A Jackson Harbor fisherman was persuaded to come cross island to Detroit Harbor to show them how to cut down a tree! The four became the nucleus of the first permanent Icelandic settlement in the United States.

Conan Bryant Eaton relied upon so many persons to help him in the preparation of this book that he found it impossible to name each one. He depended as well upon a rich variety of printed source material, carefully cited at the end of this work.

Washington Island is divided into two parts. The first is a year-by-year chronicle of major community developments beginning in 1836 and provides the reader with an accurate overview of the period covered.

Part Two is devoted to the Icelanders, that hardy band of pioneers who served as the vanguard for a sizable immigration. While Icelanders never became so numerous as to dominate the community, they prospered through immigration and inter-marriage. Readers will note that Mr. Eaton's style of writing differs here from Part One as he seeks to capture the flavor of those from a faraway land acclimating themselves to a new world.

Eaton Book Committee

Goodwin Berquist, Chairman
Kathy Findlay
Sylvia Nelson
William Olson
Rhea Sikes

Town of Washington
Historical Archives Committee

PREFACE

The pre-settlement period of this island cluster - the years before the first non-Indians came to seek a living here touched upon in the early pages of *Rock Island* and *The Naming* and in bits throughout *Death's Door,* is only briefly re-stated in this book. The present narrative runs parallel to a part of *Rock Island,* touching it or blending with it at times, as life on the sister islands touched or blended; but the focus now is on Washington Island as formerly it was on Rock. Detroit Island, another sister, plays its lesser role in the township drama as history directs.

In the Island Series' first three books we have treasured the privilege of naming all those persons and institutions who helped by contributions of historical material in our project. The greatly increased number of persons - and the terrifying possibility of omitting even one deserving name - seem now to place this pleasant indulgence beyond our reach, We cherish the hope that each such valued contributor not only knows of our deep gratitude, but takes pleasure in knowing the importance of his own contribution to the preservation of the islands' history.

In adding this book to our series we say, as did Robert Baird in the Introduction to his *Emigrant's and Traveller's Guide to the West* in 1832:

"Should any one, upon perusal, find in it nothing which he did not know before, let him lay it aside quietly, and remember that it was not written for him, but for the less informed."

C.B.E.

Washington Island
June, 1972

7

Acknowledgments

Kate West of Bethesda, Maryland designed the front cover for this publication. The book committee wishes to express its sincere thanks for her creative effort.

The maps which appear inside the front and back covers are the collaborative work of Kate, Steve Eaton and Rhea Sikes.

While most of the pictures reproduced here form part of the photographic collection of the Island Archives, we should like to recognize the loan of images from several Islanders: Lorna Bell Cornell who generously shared with us enlargements from her father's *Bell Collection*, Arbutus Greenfeldt, Sylvia Nelson, Barry McNulty and Linda Thompson.

The Book Committee wishes to express a special note of thanks to Arni Richter for his assistance in securing an early photograph of Eyrarbakki from the National Library of Iceland.

William Olson, of Jackson Harbor Press, kindly donated his time and talent in preparing this text for publication. Without him, our work would have been far more time-consuming and the result less perfect.

Finally we wish to thank Archivist Barbara Ellefson for her many helpful suggestions and Goodwin Berquist for tying it all together.

Illustrations

PART I
1836-1876

The first third of the nineteenth century brought tremendous changes to the region later to become the state of Wisconsin. The ending of the War of 1812 gave the young United States the opportunity to control and develop this vast and virgin region. In quick response the federal government built forts to house units of the army; used pen, purse, and sometimes force to subdue and remove all but scattered remnants of the Indian tribes; and vigorously set about examining, charting and subdividing this tempting land.

Meanwhile, developments beyond the realm of government produced the means and generated the pressures which could fill with human enterprise the natural condition which white men considered an abhorrent vacuum. In America's eastern states and in Europe, men looked westward for land and opportunity; the invention of the steamboat made large-scale migration possible, while a plethora of emigrant's guides praised the west country in print and pointed the way; and freshwater fishing as a source of livelihood began reaching into Lake Michigan from the Straits of Mackinac.[1]

In 1832 the flareup of the Sauk War and its quenching with the capture of Black Hawk turned the attention of emigrants to this region which within four years would gain civilized status as Wisconsin Territory, while small bands of natives still frequented isolated patches of their ancestral lands.[2]

Few such campsites were more isolated in 1833 than the Island of the Little Detroit. The Ottawa Indians there had expressed the wish to see and hear a priest and preacher of the faith in their locality, and Father Frederic Baraga came in a small canoe from the northeastern shore of Lake Michigan to seek these lost sheep. He wrote in June to his sponsors in Vienna: "May 14 was the happiest day of these poor Indians, and also for me it was one of the most beautiful days of my life. On this day I baptized 22 of these Indians. ..." He promised to return; they promised to build a small church of wood. Together they selected the place.

Late in August he wrote again: "On this second visit I had the consolation of actually finding a small chapel of tree bark, which I blessed to God on August 9 under the name of St. Vincent de Paul. ... I also blessed there a small cemetery for the burial of Christians. ..."[3]

The Indians probably moved about with the seasons. In August of 1835, as Jesse Miner tells it, they found their secluded island encroached upon by two young fishermen who had wintered there. In the night the Ottawa attacked. Neither arrows nor the round bullets of their smooth-bore rifles could penetrate the shanty's log walls; but in shooting back, one fisherman exposed himself at a small window and was killed. Soon after daylight the Indians removed their dead to Washington Island. Then the surviving white man saw the sail of a government vessel, hailed it, and was rescued. When the ship docked at Chicago, says Miner, two of his uncles were present and heard the story from the crew.[4]

Basic elements of Miner's story appear in *Sturgeon Bay Republican,* Feb. 15, 1894, "Shipped Stone in 1832," where J.E. Defaut, aged 76, tells of his being cook on the schooner *VICTORY* which rescued the surviving fisherman. Jesse Miner might have read the newspaper story, but we see no reason to question his claim that his uncles were present when the vessel docked at Chicago; differences between Defaut and Miner in the year and in some details are not surprising under the circumstances. (Some research courtesy of Stanley Greene.)

Thus the Island of the Little Detroit probably sheltered the islands' earliest Christian church, and may have been the scene of not only their first white settlement, but of their only recorded killing of a white man by Indians. Yet, despite these early signs of advancing civilization, the dragon-shaped island long remained the most nearly pristine of this group of islands.

Several months before the little frontier tragedy, plans were well afoot for the building of a lighthouse and dwelling on Pottawatomie Island at the entrance of Green Bay. (Government surveyors working in the township called the small island where the beacon was to be located "Rock.") The tribe whose name these islands had borne for nearly two hundred years was "scattering," said the *Green Bay Intelligencer*, which added "There is something connected with the emigration of these miserable, misguided creatures, from their old hunting grounds which we cannot bear to contemplate. ..." Sentiment aside, the editorial judgment of the same newspaper of fifteen months before was now manifestly true: "The barriers of distance, a forest obscurity, and the intervention of inland seas, were now overcome...and this hitherto unknown land was fairly exposed to the enterprise of American Citizens."[5] From this time onward, Indians made sporadic appearances on the islands (usually in very small numbers) well into the 1900s. But they seem to have offered little threat to incoming settlers.

1836

There was little snow in the winter of 1835-36, and the frost bit deep; it was barely out of the ground in April when Wisconsin became a Territory. Two weeks earlier Michael Dousman of Michilimackinac signed, with the government's agent, a contract to build "a Light House and dwelling House on Pottowatomie Island at the entrance of Green Bay. ... The whole to be completed in a workmanlike manner by the first day of October. ..." Built to warn sailors away from rocky shores, the beacon began almost at once to attract footloose fishermen to the relative security of its little island base, with its assurance of at least some regular communication with the outside world.[6]

1839

While Rock Island was beginning to shelter a few working fishermen another location within the township was gaining the notice of distant speculators. In January, 1839, John J. Robertson of New York State bought at the Green Bay land office Government Lot 5 in Section 25 on the bigger island - a pleasant and potentially usable half-mile of shore in the best-sheltered southwest side of Washington Harbor.

1840

Late in the following spring the remaining south shore and the inner east side of the Harbor was purchased by John Ball of Cuyahoga County, Ohio. Early land acquisition and ownership on Washington Island followed a course far more complicated by absentee owners' speculations, trading, and tax delinquency than has been generally recognized. [7]

At this same time, the General Land Office in Washington, its agent in Green Bay, and the U.S. Treasury Department, after some six months' correspondence, discovered that three-year-old Pottawatomie Light House was located, not near Washington Harbor as their records had indicated, but "on a rock detached from Pottawatomie

Island, called in the surveys 'Rock Island.' " In June the President signed the order reserving from public sale the lighthouse land; but the letters show that at least six months earlier, "some persons" had been about to attempt the purchase of either the Rock Island site or the erroneous location on Bowyer's Bluff. Clearly, changes were imminent for the lonely, tree-girdled harbor which in 1816 had been visited, due only to the weather's whims, by a shipload of soldiers.[8]

1845

In 1844 and '45 Captain Amos Saunders of Green Bay, who had dabbled a bit in Rock Island's limited real estate, disposed of his holdings there to John Boon and others.

1846

In 1846 Saunders obtained at sheriff's sale the three government lots in Washington Harbor which John Ball had owned (and which had already passed through the hands of one Daniel ˙Whitney and of a "Washington Harbour Company" apparently owned in the East). Fishermen were coming to the region in growing numbers (those Lemont, Illinois men on Rock Island for example); and with more and more books - like Increase Lapham's new one - being printed to lure emigrants to Wisconsin. the owners of desirable property were likely to prosper.[9]

An unnamed source told Anne Whitney that the Lemont men arrived "shaking with ague and using *Jayne's Ague Cure*," which was long thereafter sold on the islands as a cure-all. Miner in "Pottawatomie" mentions no illness worse than seasickness among the first Illinois group, which included his father and uncle.

The ague in the midwest's settlement period cannot be brushed aside. Escanaba's Isaac Stephenson in his

Recollections of a Long Life: 1829-1915, (Chicago, 1915), describes epidemics of "ague and chill fever" (malaria) running in virulent form through the midwest, causing many Easterners to hesitate over moving west. In 1846 and again in 1850, most people living in the vicinity of the lakes were afflicted. "It seemed to descend upon the country like a blanket ... Few escaped it. ..." The malady did not disappear entirely until about 1870, and "the only way of escaping it ... seemed to be to go north of Green Bay, beyond which latitude it did not extend into Wisconsin."

In the February 23, 1889, *Door County Advocate* Chauncey Haskell describes having a bad case of fever and ague in Illinois in the early forties. The Graham brothers told him to go to Wisconsin if he wanted to get rid of the shakes. "In '43 I came north and went to Washington Island."

1848

By 1848 steam vessels were touching more frequently at the islands. The U.S. steamer MICHIGAN, for instance, stopped in September to fix a site for a lighthouse on Pilot Island in Death's Door. Cordwood to re-fuel them was still to be had near the light on Rock Island, but factors of manpower, supply, and loading facilities dictated that Washington Island would soon become the chief supplier. (Another wooding-station was Beaver Island, and boats brought the news that Mormon prophet Strang and a few followers from southern Wisconsin had started a colony there.)[10]

The year was charged with change, at home and abroad. Conditions were bad in Europe - in Germany and Ireland especially - and emigrants were flowing from those countries to the New World. Wisconsin entered the Union, becoming an even more promising mecca for settlement.

1849

Perhaps the short-lived Indian stir out on Rock Island in '49 induced more newcomers to favor the Harbor's shores; at any rate, the government geological survey under Foster and Whitney counted fourteen fish boats at the big island to ten on Rock, and fifty fishermen against thirty. The whitefish and trout were easy to catch, easy to sell, and the price was good - and in cash; gone were the days when fish had to be shipped to Chicago and bartered for flour. barrel-for-barrel. As the century neared its mid-point, more fishermen could be expected to come, and come they did.[11]

1850

Stability was still in the future. Generated by new federal laws giving land grants to veterans and simplifying land transfers, buying and selling more chaotic than ever filled the early 1850s. Much of this was still done by absentee owners who would never enter the community's life-stream; some of it was in parts of the Island which would not open up to much human use until after the Civil War. But while the land embracing the Harbor was held in large tracts and usually by men of some means, it was lived on and worked on by a growing number of landless settlers. The shacks, sheds and docks which the forties had seen loosely scattered about the shores now formed, here and there, almost village-like clusters. In general, so long as the squatters brought muscle or skill to the fishery, they were welcome.[12]

Late in June, 1850, a little group of the islands' leaders met on Rock Island at Henry Miner's cabin (despite the presence of Miner's two-weeks-old boy Jesse). Problems of law and order, of record-keeping and property

**"Irish Village" - a cluster of homes
located at Washington Harbor**

rights were among the matters talked over. The result was the setting-up of the Town of Washington, with Amos Saunders chairman; the offices of clerk and justice fell to early Rock Island settlers Miner and John Boon.[13]

Summer gave another occasion to sail over to the older settlement. A town picnic there celebrated the State's second birthday. A few days later the Harborites heard that across Lake Michigan on the eighth of July the Mormon Strang had got himself crowned King of Beaver Island. It was bad enough that Strang and his followers hogged the fishing in that region and were probably at the root of most net-thieving and such in the northern part of the Lake. But King! Months earlier, the Green Bay paper had said the Utah Mormons were looking for converts in Denmark and other distant places. Islanders wondered how far Strang might now reach out to reinforce his "kingdom."[14]

Near Washington Harbor, it was a year of advancing civilization. The federal government authorized a new Post

Route from Green Bay to Sturgeon Bay. A lighthouse was in operation on Pilot Island. Near the beach at the south end of the Harbor a log schoolhouse was raised, and sporadic sessions of teaching began, with pupils seated on split-log benches. As Henry Miner tallied up his town census figures, he found a total population of 169. Native-born family heads numbered 32 from New York State with 13 New Englanders, 8 Ohioans and a handful of others. The foreign-born heads were a mixed bag of 9 Irish, 7 English, 5 German, 4 Canadian, 3 Scottish, and one each from Holland, Cuba and Santo Domingo. Henry needed no census to tell him that except for the two lighthouse keepers almost everyone (even Rock Island's Dr, Ellis, in a way) either worked in the fishery or helped keep it going.[15]

1851

In February, 1851, the *Green Bay Advocate* noted that on the eleventh the Governor had signed the act incorporating Door County as a separate entity. Four months later the Islanders were interested in the same paper's article:

LAKE MICHIGAN FISHERIES

Very few, we believe, are aware of the extent to which fishing is carried on along the shores of Green Bay, and the numerous islands near it. ... The principal fishing points on and near the route from Green Bay to Mackinac, are at Grand Traverse, Fish Creek, Washington Harbor, Rock Island, and the Fox and Beaver Islands. ...Here, far away from civilized life ... the hardy fisherman seeks a favorable location, cuts away the pines sufficiently to give room for his little house and for the drying of his nets, and commences his laborious and hazardous work. His life is a life of chance; chance sends him large or small "hauls"; chance regulates the visits of vessels or steamers to his little dock for the purchase of his stock; and it is a good chance which furnishes him with flour and the comforts of life as he needs them. But chance, it seems, deals well with him generally, He is hale and hearty; his fish command a ready sale in the market; and we have never seen better

Island fishermen tending their nets

pictures of cosy and contented life than those fishing establishments, with their white lake beach, their snug houses surrounded with the long lines of nets in course of drying, their little piers, the handsome boats drawn up on shore. ...

The perfect cleanliness about these establishments is worthy of note. The beach is white and clean, and thewater which drives in upon it is uncontaminated by even a particle of offal. ... The high price of fish this spring has naturally increased the force employed in the business, and stimulated all to the most active exertion, The statistics of the trade for the present year will probably show figures already exceeding those of the whole of any previous year.

While upon this subject, we cannot forbear to mention the fishery belonging to our townsman, Capt. SAUNDERS, at Washington Harbor. He has got the finest harbor on the route, and the place, with its storehouse, boarding, cooper and fish houses, has the appearance of an active little village. There is also a fine wharf, well laden with dry wood, and an ice-house, containing some forty cords of such ice as is only found in these northern waters.[16]

Islanders found this notice of their condition generally agreeable, although some felt the editor's spectacles were a little rose-colored. And - could life really be "cosy and contented" while King Strang and his Mormons controlled the Beaver Islands? Hadn't the government hauled Strang and some of his henchmen to Detroit in May and charged them in U.S. District Court with treason, counterfeiting, robbing the U.S. mail, and trespass on the public lands? Hadn't the Strangites murdered a non-Mormon fisherman named Tom Bennett in June?

Even when all of the Mormons were acquitted that summer, the Islanders were unconvinced. They remembered the copy of Strang's newspaper the *Northern Islander* which had been passed around back in May. These islands at the entrance to Green Bay, it had said, are "a fine place for a settlement", How could anyone know what those pirates might try to grab next?[17]

1852

Nature seemed determined to match the turbulence and rigors of the times. The ice, in that winter of 1851-52, came early and froze deep. When May finally saw the ice melted, high water drowned out shoreline timber of over a century's growth. But nothing hindered the flow of newcomers to Michigan and Wisconsin and to their islands, nor the speculation in Washington Island's lands. The fever of buying and selling was reflected in the transfers of 160 acres east of Washington Harbor between February 12 and March 13. For $80 John Mungan of Massachusetts (who had obtained the property by Land Warrant in the previous August) made his mark on a deed to Martin Collier of the same state. A month later Collier sold to Horatio Woodman of Boston for $100. On the same day, Woodman sold to Patrick Byrne, another Bay State resident, for $135.[18]

The land-buying of greatest importance to the community, though, was done between May and October by a Cleveland, Ohio man about ninety years old. James M, Craw (occasionally in partnership with William V. Craw) gained title to some 540 acres in the Island's north half, and was quick to begin improvements on the Harbor's west shore. Half a mile farther north, a colony of some twenty families of mixed nationalities had sprung up between Little Lake and Washington Harbor, and was even keeping a small school for its children. [19]

In summer the *Green Bay Advocate* told of sixty Norwegians immigrating to Waupaca County, and nearly as many Morman converts arriving at Beaver Island. There were stories of more thievery among the fisheries - attributed usually to King Strang's desperadoes - and the newspaper called for the Wisconsin Militia to protect Green Bay. Of Washington Island the paper reported:

Captain Saunders, the pioneer of Washington Harbor, informs us that among the improvements of that place is a new hotel which is now in course of erection, and which is demanded by the great increase of the fishing trade.

Washington Harbor is one of the safest ports on the Lakes, and is centrally situated in the fishing region. [20]

This account not withstanding Jesse Miner suggests that Saunders, the Island's first town chairman, may have murdered a hired man on the Island.

The fall brought winds which often made net-lifting impossible, and high water knocked planks off wharves and lapped at fish houses. On November eleventh the Lake was lashed by a heavy gale, and, safe port or no, Washington Harbor was a scene of disaster. Ashore and completely wrecked were a brig from Chicago and three fish-trade craft owned in the Harbor, including Mr. Craw's thirty-ton vessel, And the year took its human toll. In February old Kennison, once of Rock Island, had died in Chicago; both Henry Clay and Daniel Webster passed from the national scene; and in December Keeper Dave Corbin died at the Rock Island light he had tended for sixteen years. For Islanders, a last galling footnote to the passing year appeared in the Green Bay paper two days before Christmas; under "DISTINGUISHED ARRIVAL" it noted the passage through the city of "The Mormon Prophet, STRANG," who had recently been elected to the Michigan legislature. His power seemed to be growing without limit.[21]

1853

By 1853 Wisconsin was being widely advertised in the East and abroad. The *Green Bay Advocate* declared that five thousand pamphlets had been sent to Europe, and the legislature was hiring a "Traveling Emigrant Agent" to steer newcomers "to our beautiful State." Books describing these western lands and waters continued to flow from the presses, and often they mentioned the islands at the mouth of Green Bay.[22]

On the islands it had been rumored that Green Bay city was a station on the Underground Railway. This seemed even more likely when, almost before anyone noticed, a half-dozen Negro families turned up living and fishing around West Harbor. Old Bennett, fisherman and boat builder, was also quite a rousing preacher. Some people claimed he had been Perry's cabin boy on Lake Erie in 1813. For a time, West Harbor parents managed to induce a Miss Larson to teach school in their neighborhood, sparing children the three-mile trudge to the schoolhouse in Washington Harbor.[23]

On May 12 the *Advocate* editorialized in euphoric mood upon "Our Bay Trade." For a number of years, it said, the fish trade on the Bay and among the islands had been expanding, attracting liberal investments by men of wealth, until now it was one of the best-paying businesses in the state, its trout and white fish reaching tables all over the Union.

The past year's record results would surely be overshadowed this season, for aside from the annual addition of fishermen and the expansions of their individual businesses, we have two steam boats employed in the trade. ... One, the COLUMBIA ... stopping only at the more important ports and fisheries. ... The FRANK MOORE is exclusively confined to the fish trade running wherever on the Bay and among the islands fish are caught or supplies are wanted, These coming right to the fisherman's home purchasing his fish, and furnishing him with supplies at his door, he is greatly benefitted. ... Besides, these boats furnish an easy and facile conveyance for passengers who may desire to visit, for business or pleasure, any points on the Bay or Islands. ... The Bay itself is full of interest, and from its month to Mackinac, the hundreds of beautiful islands that dot the blue expanse of waters, presents a scene of most rare and surpassing beauty.

Four weeks later the Green Bay paper reported: "The Steamer MORTON left this place for Cleveland on

Henry, Jesse and Martha Lee Miner

Tuesday morning last. She took down 200 barrels of white fish...and is to take 1,000 barrels from Washington Harbor for Messrs. CRAW & SONS, of Cleveland. ..."

During the year the Craw holdings increased by 172 acres. Henry Miner, having bought land both on IndianPoint and two miles farther west on the Island's north shore, moved his family over from Rock. Several newcomers seemed to be made of promising stuff: dapper,well-educated little Robert Severs from England; young Volney Garrett, who had run away from home in

Illinois with three other lads named Runion, Roberts and Wellman; David and Joseph Lobdill, the latter an accomplished sailor at twenty-three, who soon got work in Craw's fishery; and middle-aged Samuel Graham, who purchased all the land surrounding West Harbor. The Lobdills and Graham were among the several newcomers from the Beaver Island region who cherished no love for King Strang. It was rumored that the latest clash between Mormon and Gentile fishermen had actually forced them to run. Some men on the islands said it was good Beaver Island was in Michigan; Wisconsin had abolished capital punishment that summer,but maybe over there Strang might yet be strung up by the neck.[24]

1854

People coming down from Green Bay in the spring of 1854 said a new political party had been started in Ripon; they were calling it "Republican." More important - Door County's first post office was about to be established at Washington Harbor, with W. P. Ranney the probable postmaster. The *Advocate's* editor saw this as a great convenience to the six or eight hundred persons living on Washington, St. Martin and Summer Islands and part of the neighboring peninsula, all heretofore "completely isolated in winter, and in summer wholly dependent upon chance opportunities for communication. ..."[25]

In June the newspaper announced: "M.E. LYMAN, ESQ., is our authorized agent for Washington Harbor, Door Co." He worked at his job, and the newspaper printed more news than ever about the islands. Some of it was lively.

EXCITEMENT AT ROCK ISLAND, DOOR CO.

James McGill, an old man, was tarred, feathered, rode on a rail, and thrown into the lake three times, at Rock Island, on Saturday last. The cause of this violence was on account of a charge made by a Mrs. MARIAH WELLSBY that

28

McGill had taken improper liberties with her daughter, a girl of 12 or 14 years. Previous to this, Mrs. W. had endeavored to kill McGill, first with a knife and afterwards with a gun. Our informant thinks that when McG. recovers from the injuries received at the hands of his lynchers, he will be able to establish his entire innocence of the charge made against him, which will place some of the Rock Island citizens in no enviable situation. [26]

Death's Door and Washington Harbor were reported in August among the locations in which the federal government was placing its new metallic surfboats for the saving of lives and property. A social note followed:

Washington Harbor has become quite a place of summer resort... there are some thirty guests there now from Chicago. A very good house for a hotel has been put up by Mr. CRAW, and it will undoubtedly become a popular place of refuge from hot weather and cholera. A piano was landed there last week by the MICHIGAN - the first one, we presume, which has found its way to the peninsula. [27]

"White House"
Built in 1854; a haven for Island visitors

The Green Bay Advocate reported cholera reached Wisconsin from Illinois in 1854. Holand identified Craw's hotel (known locally as "the White House") as "the oldest house in the county." The building served various uses until about 1925, and remained a decaying landmark (and occasional haunted house for children) until about 1950.

The Inescapable Judgment was brought to some Islanders' attention by the Reverend William B. Hamblin, who preached on the islands that summer, exhorting fifteen persons to baptism, and inspiring the founding of a Baptist church of twenty-three members.[28]

In October correspondent Lyman (who had gained the postmastership in place of Ranney) sent his paper sad news of a clinker boat owned on St. Martin now ashore on Indian Point, its occupants probably drowned in the Bay. Another item gave a more pleasant report. Roswell Baker, who lived east of the Harbor, cut a sixteen-pound head of cabbage in August; in mid-October he harvested from the same stump eighteen heads averaging two pounds each. One Baker tomato weighed seventeen ounces, one hill of potatoes yielded 125 tubers and measured three-fourths of a bushel. Baker could use the produce; by the 1855 census his family numbered thirteen,

"Yet these lands can be bought for $1.25 per acre, and are well timbered," advised "M.E. LYMAN, P.M." A week later this item appeared: "P.M. at WASHINGTON HARBOR. We learn that Mr. J.M. CRAW has been appointed Post Master...vice M.E. LYMAN removed. Mr. CRAW is a straight-forward business man and will unquestionably make a first rate officer." In 1854 the Craw clan added to its holdings 350 acres in the Island's west half. By this time Craw's sawmill was probably operating near his dock at the Harbor's west side. Around Washington Harbor in 1854 only change was certain.[29]

The news and rumor most disturbing to Islanders came from farther down Lake Michigan. Strang's own Beaver Island newspaper had brazenly announced polygamy to be required by the law of God. And while admitting to a little discontent on Beaver, the King boasted to a Buffalo paper that his island furnished 20,000 cords of wood yearly to steamers, and sold fish worth $174,000. Green Bay's *Advocate*, meanwhile, told of Mormon missionary success in Denmark, with 500 Jutlanders about to emigrate to a Mormon colony in America. Are they heading for Beaver Island? some Harborites wondered. They said "Amen" to a letter in the paper forecasting a collision between Strang's two thousand followers and their enemies - a collision in which the Mormons must fall.[30]

In November the Mormon scare flared up. Justice of the peace William Shirtleff of Little Lake hurried to consult his fellow officer Joel Westbrook in West Harbor. The northwest part of the Island was in arms, declared Shirtleff. Rumor was that a Mormon had attacked half-breed John Laframboise with a bowie knife, Mormon boats were

**Joseph Lobdell - Island sailor-fisherman-lumberman
(1856-1874)**

hovering around one of the Island's harbors; several spies had been sent to kill Joseph Lobdill.

Under Westbrook's questioning, three complainants, former Beaver Islanders, were sure only that Laframboise had seen one Mormon. But they had lived near the Strangites and knew them well; a thieving lot, unwilling to work, forced to rob for their winter's supplies. If the peace officers failed to act now, it would be too late when the Mormons burned Island houses. Although the excitement ebbed into grumbling and threats, few Islanders doubted that Strang's followers were capable of any outrage at any moment.[31]

1855

That winter's cold was bitter, its blizzards were frequent, the snows were deep; but spring came in with news of a brighter sort. The Green Bay editor reported hearing from Mr. Riggin, keeper of Death's Door light on Pilot Island. "If we don't send him the ADVOCATE he will shut Death's Door upon us the first time we pass through...thus forever barring our return. Mr. Riggin shall have the paper." Fishing, the editor stated a month later, was good down the Bay. Young Volney Garrett from Illinois married Rebecca Lee, with William Shirtleff officiating. By a special act, the Wisconsin legislature organized the Town of Washington, thus recognizing a political entity with five years of history already behind it.[32]

Town clerk W.P. Ranney was appointed to count the town's inhabitants for the Wisconsin census. Considering the fishermen's long hours on the water and the footloose character of some of the workers, no one could have made a perfect list. Finding only six bachelors among the 190 males and 128 females tallied, Ranney realized he must have missed a number of seasonal drifters in the fisheries.

Foreign-born now numbered 91, nearly double the figure of five years before; but while in 1850 they had been mostly unmarried, now many of them headed families with several native-born children. The list still ran heavily to American easterners, with a good dose of Irish and a dash of Canadian. Missing was West Harbor's Negro colony; off to the greater safety of Canada, seemed a likely reason. The single figure Ranney wished he might omit was the one of Joel Westbrook's family in the "Insane" column. Happily, though, none had to be entered under "Deaf & Dumb" or "Blind." When joshed about it later, the clerk was never able to figure out how he had come to leave his own name off the tally entirely.[33]

In April, six gallons of whiskey had disappeared from Westbrook's storehouse at West Harbor and shown up at Craw's. The blame was variously laid to skulking Mormons, to disaffected ex-Mormons, or to the Mormons' other enemies. In summer a robbery at North Bay up the county was blamed on Beaver Islanders by Joe Lobdill, who claimed he knew the boat and its owners, the same, he said, that brought Strang to West Harbor to dicker with Westbrook for that place. Around the Island Lobdill was said to be offering twenty-five dollars to men willing to go to Beaver Island and whip out the Mormons. But two thousand was a lot of Mormons, and no one was willing to go.[34]

Some Islanders suspected Westbrook of being soft on the Mormons, and the rumor persisted that he had accepted four hundred dollars down payment from Strang on his West Harbor property. There were threats that Westbrook's buildings would be burned if he dared sell to a Mormon or so much as give one a night's lodging. Meanwhile, some hay cut by the West Harbor landowner was hauled by Craw's men into the latter's barn at Washington Harbor, and Westbrook tried fruitlessly to get satisfaction.[35]

November found Sturgeon Bay about to get a post office, with Robert Graham postmaster. Island pioneers like John Boon and Henry Miner read it with interest. Graham and his Cuban-born wife Josephine had been their neighbors on Rock Island back in the mid-forties. The Green Bay paper hoped the government would soon establish a weekly route through Sturgeon to Washington Harbor, "a service much needed to accommodate a large, intelligent and enterprising class of citizens."[36]

1856

In mid-February, 1856, young Runion and Roberts tramped over from St. Martin to Craw's store for a keg of his Wig-Wag whiskey. From the shore at Dutch Town east of the Harbor the Henry Miner family saw them struggling back north eastward in a snowstorm with their laden sled. Days later justice of the peace Westbrook, crossing to Rock Island, found their frozen bodies on the ice. That same night Craw's big barn burned to the ground, losing him nearly $4,000 in building, hay, grain and other supplies. Suspicion of arson fell on Westbrook, who with his son, was taken into custody by justice Shirtleff and shipped off to Brown County jail for trial.[37]

The winter was fearfully cold, the closed season for shipping interminable. For three months the islands had no fresh supplies and no mail. Then Henry Miner took up William Nolan's offer of twenty dollars for a trip to Green Bay and back. After eight days spent mostly on the ice battling snow, wind, and cold down to thirty below, and having pitted his life against the weather's worst fury to reach Ephraim in time for Sabbath religious service, Miner dragged his sleighload of mail, newspapers, calicoes, bleached muslin and baby flannel, fishhooks and lines, jackknives and sundries into the Harbor. Jesse Miner once asked his father to name his hardest trip carrying the mail; Henry told him this 1856 trip *"stands alone in my memory never to be forgot."*[38]

Late April found shipping lanes opening."Small sail craft from Washington Harbor" brought the Green Bay editor varied news of the islands. At Death's Door a large steamer from Chicago was hard on the beach, and a sizable brig or barque from the same port was stuck in the ice where unfavorable wind would carry her onto the rocks. The recent Town of Washington election results listed eighteen officers, with William J. Nolan as both chairman of supervisors and town superintendent. Representing Rock Island on the town board was John Boon who continued as a justice of the peace; Dr. Ellis was assessor for that smaller island; two men shared the job on Washington. Joel Westbrook (awaiting trial in Green Bay) was no longer a justice; Joseph Lobdill, a leading Mormon-hater, was one of three constables, J.M. Craw and J.W. Turner fence viewers, and cooper John Camphell sealer of weights and measures.[39]

From the nation's capital the *Advocate* had word that Jefferson Davis, secretary of war, was announcing Green Bay's Fort Howard was soon to be sold. Informed Islanders claimed the fort had been built forty years before, in the same year that brought the schooner WASHINGTON and a name to the Harbor.[40]

Word came off boats putting in at the Island that King Strang had printed a history of the Mackinac region - favorable to himself and his Mormons, of course - and mentioning Washington Harbor's fishery. Proving his instability, though, was Strang's claim that a bridge was feasible across the Mackinac straits. His *Northern Islander* rag had carried a long letter from a "J. E. Wells", of

Washington Island, ridiculing the past year's Mormon scares on the Island. A handful of converts from Iceland were said to have joined Brigham Young's Utah colony; at least they had not helped reinforce Strang's kingdom.[41]

In contrast with the rigorous winter and the turbulence of the past several years, the warming days of May and early June were almost tranquil. A sentimental link with earliest Rock Island days was broken when Henry Miner and Jesse sailed over to say goodbye to departing Amos Lovejoy. And on a placid day in June six year old Jesse, exploring the beach eastward from Dutch Town, found a six foot long Indian bow.[42]

1856

Then word reached the Island - King Strang had been shot.

Within hours, enemies of the Mormons were seeking recruits throughout all of northern Lake Michigan. Joe Lobdill easily raised on the Island a posse which set out for St. Helena near the Straits, where a force was gathering for a descent on Beaver. News and rumors reached the islands daily by fishing sailers and by every larger upward-bound vessel. Strang was dead. He was alive, but not expected to recover. He was still on Beaver. He had been taken away.

The St. Helena crowd of fifty, Washington townsmen among them, swooped down on Beaver, took seven Mormons hostage, and retreated. On July third they returned with three times the force, properly armed, to find that Strang's people had removed him by boat to Kenosha on the way to his old settlement in Walworth County. He was slowly recovering, some people said. But no matter; his followers, men, women, even babies, were driven from their homes and herded onto boats with those possessions they could carry.

For a little while, Islanders were excited by the town's publicity in the Green Bay paper; "Posse of about fifty men, mostly collected at the Bay and Washington Island ... Authorities of Mackinac and Washington Harbor are forcing all Mormons to leave Beaver Island." But as July wore on, Washington Island's people found less relish in reports of victims' suffering, and less pride in their own part in it. "Complete state of lawlessness exists..." the paper said. "Mormons more sinned against than sinning ... No quarter will be shown them .... The cause of their removal was a mob ... from Mackinac and the neighboring islands ...Their history, whatever may have been their faults, is one which will excite sympathy everywhere. ..."

The newspaper's last mention of the affair came on July 17: "STRANG died from his wounds at Berlington in this State, last week." For whatever reason - whether Islanders, ashamed, shrank from public notice, or the editor suffered a change of feeling about them and their affairs - during some months forward the paper gave noticeably less attention to the islands at the mouth of Green Bay. There was no mention, for example, when the Westbrooks were acquitted after eight months in jail, and returned to the Island.[43]

1857

Water in the Lake and Bay was high in 1857 - almost the only plethora in a year of stringency. Nation-wide economic depression slowed development of new enterprise on the islands. The fisheries continued working; but for employers and laborers alike, money was tight and supplies, especially in the long, snow-burdened winter, were painfully scarce. Some families found deerskin a saving substitute for store clothes; cat and dog skins served as children's mittens; men tunneled through snowbanks from house to cattle shed; wild birds died of starvation; and diet in many homes fell to a menu of potatoes and fish.[44]

The public business, though, could never stand still. In July, Michael Kalmbach took over the post office from J.M. Craw; and when chairman William Nolan found it inconvenient to go to Sturgeon Bay in November, his two county board colleagues dutifully traveled fifty miles by foot and sailboat in December to the Island, and held the county's first productive board meeting. They levied taxes, assessed land at three dollars an acre improved, two-fifty unimproved, six dollars for pine. Expenditures were ordered to a total of $320, a bounty of $2.50 per head was placed on wolves.[45]

1858

Public affairs gained the Green Bay paper's notice on January 7, 1858:

Taxes are now being collected for the first time...around Sturgeon Bay, and also in the islands comprising the town of Washington. The attention of non-resident owners is called to the above fact, as it is time the valuable lands in Door County paid something towards the general burdens of the State and County. This shows progress, and should have been done long since. [46]

A few lsland pioneers might have informed the editor that Wisconsin had taxed Town of Washington lands, even sold some for non-payment, back in territorial days of the earliest forties.

James M. and William V. Craw, who had purchased 462 more acres in 1855 and '56, began in April of '58 to dispose of their 1800 Island acres to various investors. In the first sale it was the dock - White House - mill tract on the Harbor's west side to New Yorker Frank S. Wilson. Until late in 1863, ownership of the Craws' former holdings is clouded by apparent duplicate sales and unkept agreements.

1859

Wresting a living from the fisheries left little time for the amenities. In early June of 1859 Jacob Richter and postmaster Kalmbach's daughter Mary planned a Saturday wedding. On Thursday justice Joseph Lobdill, the chosen official, learned he must go to Green Bay on the steamer already wooding up at the dock. Threatened with a week's delay, the party's women adjusted their plans within moments, and Jacob came off the lake dressed in oilskins to find himself heading for the altar. Walis Boice of St. Martin Island and James Cornell's daughter were luckier; their wedding took place on the Glorious Fourth as planned.[47]

Between June of 1854 and September of '55, New York-born Joseph Judson Lobdill purchased forty acres at what still is called "Lobdell's Point," plus the land across Detroit Harbor lying west of Range Line and south of Aznoe roads, later to embrace "Jensenville."

In October William Nolan succeeded Kalmbach as postmaster, becoming thereby the clearing house for community news. November found the Green Bay paper reporting "Great Fishing...by means of what is termed 'pound nets'." Hundreds of barrels a day were being taken, and the Bay's steamers came in piled with them. "What effect this wholesale slaughter of fish will have upon the supply," said the editor, "another season may tell."[48]

1860

It was not to be a good Christmas at Washington Harbor. On the night of December 19, with the James McDonald family asleep, their dwelling burned. Four children died in the flames, another the next day. On the fifth of January the mother succumbed. Of the entire family, fisherman McDonald and one badly burned child remained.[49]

In May the paper reported a Green Bay shipbuilder was sending down the Bay three "remarkably fine fishing boats, built for parties at Washington Harbor" and in September the fishing business was reported thriving. Joseph Cornell and Orson Nichols caught a trout too large to weigh on their sixty pound steelyard; they thought the fish weighed some seventy pounds. Moreover, at Washington Harbor a steam mill was sawing lumber, and merchant Frank Wilson was operating the former Craw enterprises, but with limited success. [50]

Thoughtful Islanders read the 1860 federal census figures with interest. In five years population had leaped from 318 to 631. Among family heads, native born still topped the list with forty-nine, closely pressed by thirty-nine Irish and thirty-two Germans. In the matter of family size, though, it was clear the foreign-born fathers were producing new Americans (and Islanders) more smartly than were the New Yorkers and Yankees, with the Irish well in the lead and the Germans a creditable second. Still present was the sprinkling of minorities - the English, Canadians, French, a Russian, a Cuban, a Scotsman Another - Rock Island's Jim McGill - had died that year in puzzling circumstances.

Noteworthy newcomers were the thirty-three Norwegians (six families plus a bachelor and an unattached child). And somewhat expanded since 1850 were the occupations, The classic pursuits - fisherman, cooper and laborer - still furnished a living to the greatest number by far, but farmers now numbered seven, plus William Nolan, "farmer & trader". Three men were boatbuilders, two, lighthouse keepers; the occupations of sailor, clerk, blacksmith, merchant, tailor, shoemaker, housekeeper, schoolteacher each claimed one Islander. Beyond any doubt, the Town of Washington had reached a considerable state of civilization.[51]

1861

A winter of deep snows was hardly breaking up when the *Green Bay Advocate* of April 15 reached the islands with the headline:

EXCITING WAR NEWS.
THE WAR COMMENCED!
FT. SUMTER TAKEN.

Islanders, looking for no sweeping changes from a war which promised to be quickly won on faraway fields, went about their work. At a cost of fifty dollars to the public a curving road was surveyed, cut out and worked, giving residents on Detroit Harbor's east side access to the town's north and west sections. In addition, lines for five other future roads, including one on Rock Island, were run by the county surveyor. But those who looked about the island township late that fall saw that several young men (including some of Rock Island's Illinois boys) had left to join up with military units in Wisconsin or elsewhere. The town's human resources already showed erosion by the distant storm.[52]

1862

The March 27 *Green Bay Advocate* in 1862 noted having "received the first No. of the *Door Co. ADVOCATE.* ..." Among the new paper's charter subscribers were Capt. J.J. Lobdill, William Betts and Dennis McDonald. From that time onward, Islanders turned gradually to the new county paper, which might be expected to show more interest in their affairs than could the more distant metropolitan weekly. Town of Washington had, after all, more than one-fifth of the county's people.[53]

From the start, the Sturgeon Bay paper kept close watch on events affecting the islands, The Wisconsin legislature, it was reported, was asking Congress to extend the mail route from Green Bay through the county seat to Washington Island. State school money for the Town's 105 scholars (at fifty cents per scholar) totaled $52.50. Maple sugar from the Island's representative on the county board, D.H. Rice of Washington Harbor, seemed to the editor "the finest and whitest grained ever made. Over 4,800 lbs. of this delicious sugar was made during the past season, on Washington Island. ..."

The legislature, said the paper, now forbade setting any pound or trap net in more than twenty feet of water, off, under, or on the south point of any bay or inlet on the west shore of Lake Michigan in Door County, with ten to fifty dollars fine for each offense.

Under heading "Our Island Fishermen" appeared D.H. Rice's report that "recruiting has been very successful on Washington and Rock Islands; over 20 volunteers have enlisted from there. Mr. W. P. Ranney, who everybody knows to be a whole-souled patriot, has been giving $15 bounty to every volunteer from the town of Washington." The paper's October "Door County War Roll," however, reported thirteen volunteers in service from the town, but twenty-eight others "subject to draft."

For an October teacher's examination at the schoolhouse of the Island's district number one (Washington Harbor), the paper requested applicants "to provide themselves with books, pen, ink and paper." In August the *Advocate* had boasted of Door County's 100,000 acres of good farm and timber lands at fifty cents to five dollars an acre; but December brought news of "Free

Homesteads," to be had by pre-emption for actual settlement.

1863

March brought the war's first serious shock to Washington Harbor. Vermonter David Haines, who had left his wife and several children to enlist the summer before, died in a Tennessee hospital on the day his last son was born on the Island.[54]

The town re-elected D.H. Rice chairman. The *Advocate* notified the islands that Rice was its authorized agent, and the New York-born farmer responded with a suitable letter:

Washington Island, Door Co.

May 25, 1863

Dear Advocate:-We wake up once in a while, and let you know that we are amongst the living. I am happy to say that the staple business of the Islands is flourishing, wood is in good demand at improved prices, and the fish market having recovered from its long depression, is gladdening the hearts of our fisherman with better prices than ever.- We also take pride in reporting that of maple sugar, the Island has produced during the past season, (spring,) 5,800 pounds weight of such sugar as we are not ashamed to brag on. Our farmers too are busy as bees clearing up land and putting in crops, subduing the forest, and widening their farm borders constantly. To all who are homeless, and looking westward, we say come to Door County, and its lovely Islands, ... we have plenty of government lands free to settlers, of the choicest kind for soil and timber, ... no better can he found in the north western country. We have a good home market for all our produce, as fish, wood and grain, our waters abound with fish, our winters are mild, summers delightful, dame nature has lavished upon us her richest blessings, with everything

*to please the eye, and gladden the hearts of all, we all live
to a good old age for we have no doctors ; we live in peace
and unison, for we have no lawyers; so come one and all to
our Island home, where a rich harvest awaits your sinewy
limbs, and sun burnt brows, and where the evening of your
days can be spent in contentment and peace, the rewards of
righteousness and industry.* [55]

Yours. Ever,
D. H. RICE.

Early in August young Horace Beam drowned near
the Harbor while adjusting a fish boat's rigging. The news
must have taken a long time to reach his father in the Third
Wisconsin Cavalry and his mother, nursing in a military
hospital.[56]

The *Advocate* saw vessels clearing "almost every
day" from county ports including Washington Harbor, with
"lumber. shingle, bolts, cedar posts, telegraph poles, cord
wood, fish &c. &c." And it reprinted a *Manitowoc Tribune*
account of an exploring trip to Door County which said of
Washington Island:

*5,000 acres may yet be taken up under the
Homestead Act...Three harbors, considerable business, is
on the steamboat line of travel to Buffalo, and has,
perhaps, two hundred inhabitants. In the evening we held a
Union war meeting, to the edification of loyal men and
discomfiture of copperheads. Sunday afternoon we saw
three Government boats in Washington Harbor, viz: the
revenue cutter COQUETTE, and two steamers.*

The Island held some political importance. The
October 8 paper advertised the keynotes of a speech to be
made at Washington Harbor by *Advocate* publisher Joseph
Harris in his campaign for state senator:

FOR THE UNION-
DEATH ON TRAITORS-
SAVE THE REPUBLIC FROM SOUTHERN REBELS

On November 7 Willet P. Ranney paid the Door County sheriff $260 for title to the former Craw dock and business property on the Harbor's west side. Late in the month the Draft List for Town of Washington appeared: James and Samuel Love, W.J. Nolan, Thomas S. Cornell, Thomas Stinson. H. McFadden, Spencer Haines, A.J. Ward. In the whole county no town matched this number but populous Brussels, with its one draftee more.

1864

Tension gripped Islanders' households through a bitter cold January, but relaxed for some when March brought exemptions to four - William Nolan was over forty-five, Irish-born Samuel Love an alien (James was not mentioned), Cornell was now non-resident, Stinson had heart disease. Young Haines had dropped out of sight. Hugh McFadden and Alexis Ward both served, both died in Andersonville prison. [57]

Midsummer was graced by the visit of the Reverend Peter Kitwood. a preacher whose personality and message reached a goodly number of Islanders. Plans for a church building got off to a lively start. [58]

Month by month the fluctuating local draft status mingled with other news. Thirty-four were liable to the draft; ten were drafted. (The editor thought the islands had furnished volunteers enough to be clear of the draft.) Republican President Lincoln beat Democrat McClellan 230 to 33 in Door County. Fishing was over for the season; it had been very successful, with prices good.

1865

Joel Westbrook performed the marriages of James Cornell to Julia Coats and of William Cornell to Hannah Johnson. Chairman Rice moved to Sturgeon Bay, ran for county judge, saw his daughter Rosalie (who had taught Rock Island's two dozen pupils the winter before) married to Joe Harris, Jr. Patsy Flannigan and Joseph Folwell carried the mail between Ephraim and the Harbor, were marooned on Plum Island by drifting ice in the Door, lived three days on basswood buds. Safely home, Patsy said he would never carry mail again if he got one hundred dollars a trip. Draft quota for Town of Washington dropped to seven; soon afterward fourteen were drafted.[59]

The editor found early April's weather delightful. "Maple sugar is becoming plenty," he crooned. "The pigeons are flying thick, and already the sportsmen are skirmishing with them."

Two weeks later the news came by way of Chicago and Green Bay - President Lincoln was dead.

Early in that peaceful summer Door County's assessors established values for the most common taxable articles of everyday commerce:

Staves for Fish barrels per M 6.00 ... Good hard wood, on bank per cord 1.50 ... White Fish, per 1/2 barrel each, 5.00 ... Pound net new - with pound boat $600.00 ... Gill nets good - new each 4.00 ... Half barrels, for fish, .50 ... Salt per barrel, 2.50 ... Fishing boats with sails from $25 to $150 each.

Two months later the county's total real estate valuation showed a drop of about one-fourth since 1862; but Town of Washington's loss was almost two-thirds - to a mere $7,031 for the 4489 acres held by taxable owners. Personal Property (chiefly fishermen's boats, nets and other gear, plus the islands' few farm animals) totaled only $6,308 - lower than the real estate figure for the first time, thus clearly reflecting the modest beginnings of land-clearing and farming.

That summer's census put on paper what everyone well knew: in four years of war the town had dropped from 631 inhabitants to a scattered 267 - actually fewer than ten years before. Eighty were foreign-born. Business, of course, had shriveled accordingly; and some land had gone begging. For $2,000 (plus a few dollars in unpaid taxes) the Ranney brothers had gained title to five whole government lots - 240 acres - embracing Washington Harbor.[60]

Without war, there was still attrition, from garden ravaging by cutworms to Mr. Nolan's sad report to the Green Bay paper: a fish boat laden with nets was overtaken by a squall off Bowyer's Bluff and capsized, while neighbors watched, helpless. Drowned were James Love, Frank Woolf and Ed Weaver, all married, and Weaver with four children of tender age. (Love's widow wished the draft had taken him when his name was listed.) Nolan also reported: "A Norwegian who moved to the Island last spring, with his family, has disappeared, and it is thought he has committed suicide, as he was subject to fits of insanity."[61]

Quite a few former Islanders came home from the War, others who had never lived in these parts drifted to the islands, and some came directly from abroad often to join relatives here. Over on Rock two veterans from Maine took over the lighthouse - one-legged Abe Capers as keeper and Abe Grover assistant. There were gratifying homecomings other than soldiers'; the Reverend Mr. Kitwood returned, bringing aid from the Seamen's Friend Society plus the promise of his own presence for a year or so. With this encouragement a group of Islanders framed up a spare clapboard meeting house with hand-split shingle roof, and named the church "Bethel."[62]

**Non-denomonational Chapel (1865)
now part of Bethel Church**

1866

Early in 1866 the Post Office Department advertised for offers to carry the mail between Ephraim and Washington Harbor monthly from November first to April thirtieth. Meanwhile, Martin (Ole) Oleson left the Island with mail on March eighth, started back from Eagle Harbor the same day, was never heard from again. It was supposed he fell through a crack in the ice and drowned.[63]

Three days after the courier's disappearance, Tom Stinson's wife died, leaving ailing Tom with several children. A week later John Boon died on Rock Island. "One of the oldest settlers in Door County, and the oldest on the Island, having arrived on Rock Island in 1836, he was a man much esteemed by all who knew him" pronounced the *Advocate*. Some sixty-odd Washington Islanders took a day off and crossed to Rock for the burial.

In another week to the day, the Kenwards lost their eleven year old Sarah. It was generally felt to have been a bad spring on the islands.

J.J. Lobdill took over as postmaster. Maple sap was scant, though there was always enough sugar for mothers to wrap in a bit of muslin for pacifying the baby. Island housewives who saw the *Advocate* could read of the advertised Universal Family Sewing Machine and the Little Giant Clothes Wringer, but for most of them dreams of owning these marvels were hopeless unless the new firm just going into the fish trade in competition with the Ranneys should bring about a better price to the fisherman.

That hope was short-lived. The August paper that carried Island news of "a picnic by the school children" also noted that fishing was not very good, and the price had fallen. But there were interesting outside developments. Nearly six and one-half million acres of Wisconsin lands were proclaimed for sale by the government; and the *Advocate* advertised the offering of capital stock in the Sturgeon Bay and Lake Michigan Ship Canal and Harbor Company. The Island's Reverend P. Kitwood was announced as its representative on the Republican Party's Union County Committee. Island men cast 41 votes in the November elections; the sloop FLASH went ashore in a northwest blow; a real snowstorm hit late in the month; and two weeks before Christmas it was really winter, the Bay already partly frozen over.[64]

1867

The *Advocate* reported in January: "Mr. D.E. Ranney has been appointed Postmaster at Washington Harbor, in place of Mr. J.J. Lobdell, who failed to send his bond to the Post Office Department." By late May, the job had passed to Hiram A. Knowlton.

The Islanders, having shipped over 20,000 barrels, could look back on the past year's fishing as tolerable despite ups and downs. But nothing was perfect. An 1866 law providing for a State Fish Inspector, said the paper, "has been amended so as to be as much of a nuisance to fishermen as possible." Before packed fish was removed from the county it must be overhauled, inspected, repacked, resalted and branded by the Inspector or his deputy, all at a fee of ninety cents a barrel. Moreover, all barrels must be well hooped with ten good hoops. From Nolan's dock on the east side to Ranney's on the west, muttering was heard around Washington Harbor, some of it salted with Irish profanity.

With Bethel's congregation numbering a solid fifty-six, the Reverend Mr. Kitwood relinquished the pulpit to the Reverend Mr. Willard, who was followed in autumn by the Reverend Mr. Bristol. A half-dozen Islanders fell delinquent in their personal property taxes; the smallest amount was fifteen cents, the largest less than twelve dollars. But all in all it was a pleasant summer, and when the *Advocate's* editor visited Washington Harbor aboard the little steamer SARAH VAN EPPS on a fresh August morning he was moved to report "Everything was lovely there. ..." On a day in late November Tom Stinson's boy stumbled breathlessly down to Washington Harbor with shocking news his father had been shot dead. The chaos of the next few hours made it hard for anybody to keep events straight; and Islanders generally thought the *Advocate* a week later summed up the story passably well:

Murder at Washington Island.
Last Sunday PATRICK McDONALD of Washington Island was lodged in the County jail to answer for the murder of THOMAS STINSON of the same place. The following are

the facts of the murder and the cause that led to it, as near as we can ascertain:

Some months ago STINSON hired a yoke of cattle of McDONALD. While the cattle were being used by S. by some accident one of them was hurt and rendered useless. It was killed and sold by S. The other ox was returned to McD. and the matter ran along for sometime without a settlement until finally the two men got into a difficulty with each other and S. refused to pay for the ox, even alleging that he had never hired it, and procuring his brother to swear to that fact. Upon this a warrant was taken out for the arrest of the brother on a charge of perjury and one for S. On the charge of subornation of perjury. The brother made his escape from the Island. At the same time McD. commenced a suit against S. for the recovery of the value of the ox killed and a steer belonging to S. was taken possession of by the officer and McD. S. went and took the steer from the custody of the officer and killed it, the justice deciding that as it was meat for the family of the defendant it could not be again attached.- On the 22d inst., the day of the murder, S. was at work killing and dressing the steer at his place and McD. was heard in loud and angry altercation with him by a person passing by. A short time after S.'s boy, who was working in a field a short distance from the scene of the murder, heard the report of a gun and running towards the place where the sound came from, found the body of his father stretched dead on the ground beside the body of the steer. He at once went to Washington Harbor to raise an alarm. A Mr. SMITH who was also near, heard the report of the gun and discovered the bloody evidence of murder just after the victim's son had gone. An alarm was at once raised and a party proceeded to the house of McDONALD and he was arrested within two hours after the deed was committed. It was found that McD's gun had been loaded with powder and seven buck shot, corresponding with the seven shot holes found in the murdered man's breast. On his arrest, McD. also acknowledged that he had shot at STINSON and said that if S. was dead he was glad of it.

There were, of course, some who claimed personal knowledge and who disagreed sharply, not only among themselves, but with certain details of the published account. As time went by, though, one variation became accepted as absolute fact on the islands: It was really Dennis McDonald who did the shooting. But Pat, mindful of his brother's bigger family, had shouldered the blame.[65]

Henry Miner house; site of Island post office in 1867

War veteran Henry Miner came back from Illinois with his family and built a small cottage above the Harbor's southeast shore. It was natural that the postmaster's job (its accounts badly tangled up by three incumbency changes within the year) should seek him out. With the annual salary now stabilized at ten dollars, people hoped things would be set for a while. No government provision was made for carrying the mail in winter. Islanders naturally looked again to Miner for that, especially for a trip before Christmas.

On the twenty-first Miner borrowed an old canvas-patched lighthouse boat and left Detroit Harbor for Ephraim with a northeast snowstorm gathering force. By Christmas morning he was still unheard from. Then seventeen year old Jesse, skating on Washington Harbor's two nights' ice, saw in the distance the flapping ear laps on his father's fox-skin cap. Henry was drawing a borrowed hand sled loaded with mail.

Someone shouted, "Here's the December mail. Three cheers for Miner!" Before Henry reached the postoffice half the mail was handed out and on its way about the Island.[66]

1868

Of great interest in March was Pat McDonald's two-day trial, which the *Advocate* called "the sensation of the late term of Court." Pat was found guilty. The defense cited irregularities in the handling and conduct of the jury, and after a day's argument the judge ordered Pat to the Brown County jail to await a new trial in July.

Few Islanders knew that in May two Danes named Saabye and Andersen bought government lands near the very middle of the Island. But those Danes and the handful of their countrymen who arrived during the year and attacked the Island's interior forests with axes gave impetus to the slow growth which the community had shown since the War. And the older settlers eventually gave them a generous welcome; blind Grandma Cornell, for example, gave little Christian Saabye a pair of woolen mittens of her own knitting, and Ranney's store extended much-needed credit.[67]

In early summer the new county school superintendent, visiting the Island's log school on the Washington Harbor beach, found sixty-six pupils enrolled, but an average attendance of only thirty-five. "School house old and unfit for use," he reported; "the south-end has no window and is very close and warm. Miss Ethel Pomeroy of Appleton, has charge ... and with a little more attention to discipline will make an excellent teacher. Average age of pupils less than 7 years." The annual school meeting voted to raise $300 for teacher's wages and $500 to build a new schoolhouse.[68]

After a scorching spell in July, Pat McDonald's case came up in the circuit court. Pat's counsel claimed the judge's prejudice precluded an impartial trial. The case was removed to Dodge County, and the sheriff set off with the prisoner for the jail in Juneau, Wisconsin.

The mid-October paper which reported the year's worst storm - cold rain turning to snow in a northwest gale that made houses shake - also told that Pat had been found guilty of murder in the first degree. The county superintendent reported 134 children between four and twenty in Town of Washington; clearly, about half were not enrolled in school. Fifty-one men voted in the election which made U.S. Grant President. The *Advocate*, noting that this was less than full voting strength, estimated the town's population at 364, up 97 from 1865. But local leaders knew that a true count of the newcomers - the non-voting Danes and Norwegians back in the woods - would raise it still higher.

1869

A March, 1869 *Advocate* announced the passing of town government from Chambers Island. The Islanders in Town of Washington, though, saw on their islands a well-functioning political, economic and social structure. There was no dearth of candidates for the eleven offices to be filled at the April election; but education, they could see, had not kept pace with other progress. For only twenty days in the past season Charles E. Bradner had taught in the old log schoolhouse near the water, and attendance was small. The annual school meeting in September voted another $450 to complete the modern frame schoolhouse Dane L.P. Ottosen was engaged in building, and threw in $100 for teacher's wages. The outmoded old log building would be kept for a wood shed.[69]

**Schoolhouse Beach School (c. 1870)
moved inland to protect children from drowning**

Dr. Ellis of Rock Island moved away from the town, leaving Islanders (when they had time to think about it) with an uneasy, unprotected feeling. To old timers like the Miners, the little neighboring island had become a ghost of its lusty self of twenty years before; but the big island was developing and gaining vitality month by month.[70]

On November 2, Jesse Miner accompanied his father on the first mail carrying trip paid for by the federal government - and suddenly the days were past in which Islanders chipped in a dollar or so a winter for the carrier. Henceforth, the mail would move twice a month to Ephraim by carrier in winter and spring, weekly to Green Bay by steamboat in summer and fall. In another transition, Bethel pastor Bristol entrusted his flock to newly-arrived Curtis G. Lathrop, who impressed many Islanders from the first as a reassuringly capable man who showed an active interest in the resurgent community.[71]

1870

At times in the early months of 1870 the temperature touched a bitter minus fifteen; yet the *Advocate* reported fishing light at the Door due to poor ice. Another item was more pleasant: "Expenses of the town of Washington...did not exceed $60 during 1869. That's a good town to move to." Islanders knew, of course, that this covered only town government; school, county and state levies boosted their total tax levy just over $1100.[72]

The March 3 *Advocate* was of special interest. "DOOR COUNTY: Its Advantages" was the heading of a long article listing the many inducements offered by the county to immigrants and to capital. As they faced a fresh decade, some Islanders found it appropriate to compare their lives and prospects with those so glowingly described in print.

Like the rest of the county, it was said, the town still contained lands to be sold by the State at about one dollar an acre, and some which the federal government would parcel out as 160 acre homesteads for ten dollars plus the work of improving them. Schooling was free to all though already this was proving an expensive effort for the Island.

Log cabins were the typical first homes of homesteaders

In fishing for whitefish and trout the Town of Washington took a back seat to no one, but logging was advanced in the county well beyond what the Islanders were cutting, and Island maple sugar-making stood far below its onetime level.

Certain matters of legal fact in the paper were news to most people, and reassuring - to the poor especially. Largely safe from seizure for debt in Wisconsin were not only a family's 40 acre home place with buildings, a good yardful of livestock, tools, implements, furniture, but also a sewing machine, the family Bible, a seat or pew in a place of public worship, and the right of burial of the dead. Exemptions from taxation, too, were reasonably generous.

The advantages Door County offered to a poor laborer or mechanic were brightly contrasted in the paper with the onerous struggle for existence in Europe; and the glorious rights and freedoms which blessed the holder of American land made almost unthinkable the feudal oppression of the Old World. To the Island's handful of Danish newcomers and to the relatives in Europe to whom they might write, the long dissertation on the county's attractions boiled down to this: "Farmers are the owners of the land they cultivate. ... Land can be obtained almost without price. ... A hearty welcome will be extended to every person coming here to help build it up."[73]

Fifty-two men attended the town meeting in April. Their most unusual action was the election of a clergyman, Bethel's Reverend Mr. Lathrop, as town chairman. In June, the leading younger citizens received credit when the *Advocate* printed the county's Honor Roll of "scholars who have been correct in deportment, regular and punctual in attendance and perfect in recitations. ..." Jesse Miner, now just twenty, and town treasurer Pete McBride's daughter Mary represented the Island.

In the last days of June, Michigan's State Geologist Alexander Winchell sailed about among the islands, entering in his notebook his own trained observations, and some locally-acquired information of varying accuracy:

(Camp) 25 June 1870 Detroit Harbor, Washington Island. I am told by ___ Souci, a Frenchman who fishes from this harbor in Lake Michigan and who owns 300 acres of land at this place that there are about 300 fishermen on the island and about 100 boats. They are "Yankees", Irishmen, Germans, and Danes. He is the only Frenchman on the island. A settlement of several families of Danes and Norwegians is on the west side of the island. They are farmers principally.

There are numerous other farms on the island. Washington Harbor is exactly (north) from our camp. There are vague rumors of marble on the island. ...

...Monday 27 June 1870. Washington Island. South of West Harbor. An outcrop of Niagara limestone ... Will make a valuable building stone. Also would make oilstones.

Washington Harbor, (Camp) Monday 27 June 1870 A threatening thunder cloud and gale of wind approaching drove us into an early camp in this beautiful little harbor. Propellers between Buffalo and Green Bay make regular stops at this harbor, taking away great quantities of fish. Ranney & Co. are the buyers and shippers.

Here I find numerous fishing boats, whose owners are just now considerably agitated about the annual boat race to come off at Beaver islands July 4th. It is expected several fishing boats from this place will compete for prizes. ...

Washington Harbor village is much scattered about the bay, and contains but two or three good houses, one church which also answers for a schoolhouse, postoffice, store, fishermen's houses, cooper shops & ware houses for inspecting and repacking fish.

... Tuesday 28 June 1870 In the morning I visit "the mountain." ...

... McBride's quarry.

Washington Island. A man by the name of __ McBride has opened a test quarry on the east side of Washington Harbor...he finds a crystalline, gray, unfossiliferous rather coarse-grained limestone, which he is encouraged to call marble.

... Jackson Harbor, Washington I ... One fishing establishment is located here.[74]

In August, the *Advocate* reported the Island's fishing the poorest in fourteen years, the largest known haul being eleven salt barrels of fish from a gang of twenty-eight nets. James Sanford of the Harbor, sailing toward the fishing ground, helplessly watched as the schooner TEMPEST of Chicago bore down on his boat and struck her amidships, breaking his foremast and jib boom, throwing himself and his man into the water from the capsized boat, and losing him nineteen new nets. In hard times, no fisherman with wife and seven children deserved this.

Coincidentally with increasing farming had appeared the first serious threat of potato bugs (driven across Green Bay by winds, the editor surmised). The paper suggested Paris Green plus flour or dry wood ashes, dusted on the dew-covered vines.

From the Green Bay paper, the *Advocate* copied the "Sad case" of the Harbor's fisherman Ira Westbrook, who brought to the Bay on the propeller ROCKET his wife, "a raving maniac ... Insanity is caused ... from meeting her father and brothers who came unexpectedly to see her after being absent many years ... Several small children ... are thus suddenly left without a mother's care."

Island chairman Lathrop preached at a Sturgeon Bay church on the text: "Set your affections on things above, not on things on the Earth." The paper reported the edifice well-filled, the discourse admirable.

The summer brought Islanders a good chance to compare current conditions with those burgeoning times before the War. The federal census as of June first showed that population had struggled back from its post-war 267 to 385 still far below the 631 of 1860. Among adults, native-born easterners (especially New Yorkers) still formed the community's backbone; but five family heads now claimed Wisconsin as their birthplace. Danes, in their first appearance in the federal listing, outnumbered Irish family heads by one and Norwegian by two, though the Irishmen's big families added up to 71 persons against the Danes' 49 and Norwegians' 42. Already the name "Fagerwick" - "Beautiful Bay" - was attached to the Danish settlement in the Detroit Harbor region. Seven German households with 47 persons now held the fertility laurels for two reasons: Germans were unique in having no adult male without wife and children; and lightkeeper Rohn and fisherman Irr were doing their full share, with eight children and ten.

Fishermen plus attendant coopers, laborers, and a "gill net knitter" still dominated the listings; four females appeared as "domestic servant"; Joseph Lobdill now called himself "lumberman"; the perennial "Light-House Keepers"were present; the avowed farmers had increased during the decade from eight to only ten. (The *Advocate*, though, analyzing the census that fall, credited the entire Town of Washington with 69 dwellings, 13 farms, and 189 acres cleared.) Livestock were few, total crops and farm products meager; clearly, the Island had barely begun to blend farming with its thirty year old fishing economy.[75]

Cutting wood and hauling logs to the dock for export

The county superintendent's annual report showed that school had been kept 146 days in the Island's one formally-established school district; 63 male children and 62 female were counted, aged four to twenty. At the light on Rock Island, Abe Capers died, leaving wife Paulina to rear eight children on a veteran's pension; assistant keeper Grover turned to fishing. William Betts, assisted by fellow veteran and fellow New Yorker James Fuller, took over the lighthouse. Widow Boon and the Silas Wrights had left Rock Island during the year.[76]

John O'Neill's boys saw their little fishing steamer KITTY GAYLORD launched at Green Bay and took advantage of the unusually mild November which helped stretch navigation into the longest season in years and brought in hauls of remarkable size. This "novel experiment" as the *Advocate* called it, moved the Harbor's Ranney & Shipman to order a 56 footer of KITTY's type; Delbert Ranney and partner Enos Bradner contracted for a 52 footer; and former Rock Islander Robert Graham in Sturgeon Bay began getting out timbers for a similar craft. The little tug's waves reached as far as St. Martin and Beaver Islands, where steamers were begun. The O'Neills had brought to Lake Michigan something really new in the fishing business.[77] Meanwhile, the Danes were gradually expanding their holdings. A William Wickmann of Milwaukee found Jim Fuller willing to part with his 61 acre homestead on Detroit Harbor and they closed the deal for $400: a few fish nets went with the land. Wickmann was said to be partners with an Icelander, one of four Wickmann brought to the Island late in the fall. But aside from one of the McDonald boys, who gave them pointers on using an axe in the woods, few Islanders knew the newcomers by sight.[78]

1871

Postmaster and carrier Henry Miner was asked by some Island smokers and chewers to replenish their tobacco stock on his next trip with mail. Miner's strict moral scruples made him refuse. Son Jesse carried freight for six cents a pound, he said; they could deal with him. On Henry's next trip to Ephraim he found over 100 pounds of tobacco in the mail. The addressees paid the government sixteen cents a pound in postage; the well-burdened mail carrier earned not an extra penny for hauling it fifty-two miles on the ice.[79] Miner hauled the tobacco only the twenty-six miles home from Ephraim, but this was insult enough. His son Jesse wrote some forty-five years later in his "mail carrying" manuscript: "It was not safe to say tobacco to Him for six months & a day. ..."

The new town board embraced two New Yorkers and a Scot, with other offices held by two more York Staters, a Dane. German, Canadian, Prussian. The county clerk received a bill for $500.10 from Dodge County for trying the McDonald-Stinson case.[80]

With the ice out, the Goodrich Line's propeller TRUSDELL began entering Washington Harbor every Tuesday and Saturday. Teacher William Gibson's thirty pupils had near-perfect attendance at April's four days of school, and with nine on the county's Roll of Honor, far outshone the other townships. Sessions continued through the summer perhaps accounting for the high teacher's salary of $500 in the school district's annual report in September.[81]

During the many years in which the Island was served by various steamship lines, winter's isolation and the open season's dependable, cheap and sometimes luxurious service from Island docks to distant Great Lakes cities were in striking contrast. In 1876, Goodrich Line steamers offered the 277 miles between Chicago and the Island, including meals and berth, for seven dollars. Nearly a century later, public (and most private) transport between these points compares badly in all respects but speed.

Newspapers continued praising the new steam fishing boats. When a man from the government's Commission of Fish and Fisheries toured Lake Michigan's northern shores in an open boat late that summer, he found the "Door Islands" notable for their use of a few steamers and large sailboats in gill-net fishing. He reported fishermen generally, considering the hardships and exposures incident to their calling, "singularly free from the habit of hard drinking."

The west shore of Green Bay was the great pound-net region of the lake, with about ninety in use the past season. Sturgeon frequently troubled by the parasitic lamprey eel were found to come into the nets in great numbers, but were thrown upon the offal heap. Trout and whitefish, mainstays of the gill net catch, showed an evident decrease in recent years, both in size and numbers. (Early in the year, though, 12-year old George Irr had caught a 36 pounder.) Three times as many nets now were fished as formerly - nets of fine linen twine in place of the old coarse cotton, and with less success. But the fishermen made a surprising haul that season; from the schooner WINFIELD SCOTT, a total wreck on Hog Island, they salvaged the entire cargo of good lumber.[82]

Midsummer saw the town fathers responding to landowners' petitions by laying out several new roads, the longest of which began well north of the Bethel meeting house, ran southeasterly around the cemetery and toward the Island's middle, then south on the range line all the way to Detroit Harbor. A shorter road made it easier to reach Henry Miner's post office from the south. Men working on the roads or in fields that summer and fall breathed a good deal of dust; the season was unusually droughty.[83]

The Reverend Curtis Lathrop relinquished the Bethel pulpit and left the Island; his daughter's playing on the reed organ was missed. Green Bay and Sturgeon Bay papers forecast - and even reported - a large influx of Icelanders; what turned up during the year was a scant half dozen (including minors), who showed little promise of success in the rugged new environment. October brought disastrous fires to Door County, to the Peshtigo area west of the Bay, even to far-off Chicago.[84]

Town chairman Volney Garrett and Peter McBride left the Island to look over opportunities in the outside world; their seats on the town board were filled by Emil Miller and William Betts. Island men cast thirty-three votes in the election for governor. Most important to landowners was the county board's assessment of lands in Town of Washington at two dollars an acre.[85]

1872

The April town meeting voted to raise fifty dollars for a poor fund. Henry Miner and teacher George Larson tied for town clerk; John O'Neill drew lots and Miner won.

**Shallow draft schooners like this
carried cordwood to other ports**

Rock Island lightkeeper William Betts was elected town chairman. Not until June did the town board find this blending of chores contrary to statute and appoint Volney Garrett - now back on the Island - in his place.[86]

In mid-year the *Advocate* cited a *Kewaunee Enterprise* article describing a steamer trip around the Door County peninsula. The correspondent (a Mr. Read) observed:

Washington Island has a population of about 300, which mainly depends on the fisheries for support, though a few good farms are being opened up. W.P. and D.E. Ranney have a store at Washington Harbor and buy fish extensively, shipping about 200,000 packages per annum. Two small tugs...ply the neighboring islands in the fish trade. There is also considerable wood and timber stuff got out here, and G.M. Wing has opened a quarry. ...[87]

Methodist minister M.M. Stolz and family came to visit the Island in August and found their stay prolonging itself indefinitely. County Surveyor James C. Pinney (assisted by Henry Miner and Jesse) completed surveying several roads previously agreed upon by the town board, including a magnificently long and straight north and south route linking Detroit Harbor with the west side of Washington Harbor.[88]

Heavy October storms put eight vessels ashore in the Death's Door vicinity, several looking like total losses. Sixty-two male and seventy-six female children were listed as of eligible age to attend the frame school house on the beach. Islanders cast thirty-one votes in the presidential election; the referendum concerning building a bridge at Sturgeon Bay tallied twenty-nine Island votes - all "No."[89]

Some baker's dozen of new Icelanders reached the Island by way of Milwaukee; most were lodged near Detroit Harbor by Wickmann and Gislason and the men were at work in the woods when winter came. As year's end approached, the county faced cutting winds and temperatures which hung steadily near twenty degrees below zero.[90]

On the day after Christmas, the *Advocate* printed parts of a chilling December 4 letter from Volney Garrett at Washington Harbor:

I was detained one week at the Door, waiting to get across. When I reached the Island I found the small pox raging fearfully in our midst. There had been six deaths, and many families were yet sick with it: school was suspended and everything bearing a gloomy aspect. Mr. Miner, the Postmaster, and his son Jesse, have both got it. Mr. Miner is out of danger, but Jesse is yet very bad. Old Mr. McFadden died at my house with it before my arrival, and all my family except one caught it, they being vaccinated had it light, and were nearly well when I got home; yet I did not enter my own house until five days after my arrival upon the Island, and the infection was all cleaned out of the premises. So I have not yet been exposed. [91]

1873

By late January, the paper could report that the pox had ceased its ravages at Washington Island; of the six who died, all were children but one.

Men's affairs went on. At rocky Hedge Hog or Porcupine Bay near the mainland's tip, a Mr. E. Gill was building a dock of cribs. Island school teacher William Gibson was elected town chairman; and Jesse Miner, now recovered and nearing his twenty-third birthday was made a justice of the peace.

When the Goodrich Line's TRUESDELL - the season's first vessel - entered the Harbor in May, several of the previous fall's young Icelanders were waiting to leave;

but a few others seemed to have taken a liking to the Island despite the bitterly hard winter.[92]

In early summer, a correspondent of Milwaukee's *Journal of Commerce* paid the Island a brief visit: his description of the town soon appeared in the *Advocate,* giving Islanders another look at their community through an outsider's eyes - all based on a landing at Washington Harbor and a four mile walk on a grass-grown road through the interior. The journalist found "a Sunday stillness" prevailing, varied by the tinkling of cow bells, which every cow seemed to wear. At a bend in the road he came upon a small white church, almost hidden in foliage, wearing a simple spire with a gilt ball. A little farther on was "the cabin of a maker of wooden shoes and carrying a jug, then some children gathering wild strawberries." The crack of an axe occasionally sounded from the tall woods, and the visitor encountered on the trail a section of pine trunk five feet in diameter.

The clearings were mostly made by Danes; the little farms showed typically a log dwelling house and another building for tools, provisions and perhaps animals. He was told there were fourteen such farms on the Island, of fifteen to twenty-five acres each; the crops of grain and fruits were said to be good.

He was disappointed in not finding the colony of Icelanders he had expected and was told that only one such remained - a fisherman on Detroit Island. The others were said to have moved on, leaving behind a good reputation; they were so polite, the schoolmaster told him, that the other people used to laugh at them.

At the dock in Washington Harbor, the Island's "metropolis," the reporter saw the store and warehouse of D.W. Ranney, seemingly the only merchant and principal proprietor of the place. On the steep hillside were clustered fifteen or twenty weather-beaten, gray cottages and dry houses with stone chimneys. The Ranney residence, a large white house with a piazza, looked out prominently among them. Piles of cord wood filed the foreground, and on the dock stood rows of fish barrels just delivered from the steamer. Half a dozen fishing boats were tied to a smaller dock built up with picturesque fish houses of logs and bark, and easterly across the harbor were more boats and scattered gray houses.

The population, including Detroit and Rock Islands and even St. Martin's, was estimated at between 250 and 300, with the greater number engaged in "gill" or "pound net" fishing. Mr. Ranney estimated for him that during the past year Islanders had got out 2,700 cords of wood, 3,500 telegraph poles, 25,000 cedar posts, and about 13,000 packages of fish. From 5,000 to 7,000 barrels of salt and 8,000 half barrels were sold per annum, the merchant told him.[93]

Pound net fishing for herring
part of Island's principal industry

Ranney seems not to have divulged a pending deal: the *Advocate* in early September reported the Ranneys' sale of their "extensive fishing establishment and store" to John Furlong of Milwaukee, who took possession immediately. The property excluding the stock of goods in the store but including the Ranneys' lands around the harbor shore sold for $10,000. The same paper corrected the report that all Icelanders but one had left, and promised: "Thirty families more, of the same nationality, are on their way ... to permanently settle on the Island." Fishing, said the *Advocate*, had been extremely good, "all of the fishermen reaping a rich harvest." Mentions during that fall of poor business conditions nationally, and use of the word "panic" in a November issue seemed to have slight application to life on the islands.[94]

1874

In fact, things were generally booming. Despite low prices for fish, in late winter buyers' teams were waiting at the elbows of fishermen on the ice to purchase the catch. In January weather ranging from stinging cold to rain and sleet, Furlong's workmen were already extending and repairing Ranney's old dock in the Harbor, and Furlong was reported to have bought all of St. Martin's Island and four or five sections on Washington. By March he had purchased in Detroit the steam yacht EMMA DYER for use in the fishery.[95]

The extent of pound net fishing at the time is suggested by the number of Islanders who appeared before justices of the peace to file "*Fishing Claims*," which were then registered in the courthouse exactly as were deeds to land, Typically, the fishermen "*inscribed*" their names on "*monuments*" of timber which they erected near the beach "*for the purpose of claiming the water outside in Green Bay for fishing with a pound net.*" Filing in 1874 were:

John M. Boyce; S. Gunderson and B. Lind; Andrew lrr and Ferdinand LaBack; Patrick O'Neill and Loyal Baker; and Hugh O'Neill, who used the schoolhouse on the beach as a bearing in describing the location.

With business activity came new facets of civilization, some popular, some not. The town meeting resolved "that a fine of $50.00 be imposed on any person shooting or killing deer in the Town of Washington within the next three years." Islander Curtis Johnson recollected that a long while back, Volney Garrett and the other old-timers, finding the Island bereft of deer, agreed on no-hunting. A doe and three fawns came over from someplace and multiplied, and we've had deer ever since.

The town fathers saw so great a need for better communication among the several developing neighborhoods that they ordered from John Furlong a twelve dollar road scraper. Late in the year, the *Advocate's* editor remarked: "Washington Island has improved very much this season, some fourteen new buildings having been put up and other improvements made."[96]

1875

In early February, a spirit thermometer on the Island indicated 40 1/2 degrees below zero, which may have suggested second thoughts to Goodlet Goodletson. The veteran of both army and navy service in the Civil War and former town treasurer had just won the U.S. mail-carrying contract; for $109 he was now obliged to carry mail twice a month from Ellison's Bay to Washington Harbor, December to April.[97]

The April town election produced a remarkable political change. Excepting clerk Robert Severs and justice Henry Miner and if one counted Icelandic highway overseer John Gislason with the Scandinavians, every office gained a Scandinavian incumbent. The three man board of

71

supervisors was solidly Danish, with William Wickmann as chairman.[98]

The new town fathers continued laying out roads with vigor, notably one beginning at the water on the west side and following the town line eastward for three miles. In August the board reacted to community change and development by slicing the Island horizontally, Lake to Bay, on a line half a mile north of the town line. Land lying south of the line, they decreed, "shall hereafter constitute School District No. 2 ... for all purposes whatsoever."[99]

Meanwhile, long-established district Number One celebrated the end of the summer term with a "pic nic." Outdoor eating, in fact, was much in fashion. The Goodrich line's propeller steamer DE PERE brought from Escanaba a party of excursionists who emptied their hampers in the picnic grounds on the hill above Furlong's dock. The July Fourth picnic in the Bethel church grove had stressed brotherhood with Scandinavian newcomers, thankfulness for divine blessings, and the benefits of life on a temperance island, where existed no licensed saloon.[100]

The Fourth was not all church picnics. It was to be celebrated by "firing of guns and crackers, boat-riding, and ball-playing. - The St. Martin's and Washington boys ... at bat and ball. In the evening, the 'light fantastic toe' will be tripped by the gay and happy. ..."

St. Martin - or St. Martin's - Island (today a distant bit of scenery northeast of our islands) quite evidently had close family, social and business ties with Washington and Rock Islanders in the nineteenth century's latter half. Censuses show St. Martin having 101 inhabitants in 1870, 77 in 1880.

Into this midsummer Eden at least one small metaphorical serpent might have been expected to wriggle. Fishing had started slowly, then surged in June, when the O'Neills dipped ninety-nine and a half packages from one haul of the pound net, leaving twenty kegs more for the next day. Other fishermen did nearly as well; and as many as seven trading vessels anchored in the Harbor at various times to dicker with fishermen for the catch, paying in cash, provisions or clothing. "Much to the disgust of our best citizens," the Island's correspondent F.E.L. lamented, "one of the vessels has seen fit to anchor near the beach and deal out that 'firey' liquid which makes men foolish. … Were it not for this vessel … bringing it here the Washingtonians might be said to be a THOROUGHLY temperate people."

The Wisconsin census credited Town of Washington with 220 males and 181 females as of the first of June; (somehow the *Advocate* printed this as 222 and 191 totaling 412). In any case, at four dollars a hundred

"Icelandic Castle"
private dwelling which served as Icelanders' first home

names, town clerk Robert Severs was sixteen dollars richer for the listing. The town's assessment roll showed livestock numbers virtually unchanged, while all thirteen gold and silver watches had disappeared from the roll in the past year; and the town listed the only shares of bank stock assessed in the county.

Near the southeastern extremity of Detroit Harbor, several Icelanders joined in framing up a tall two story dwelling to shelter newcomers until they could build houses of their own. Before long some Island wags were calling it the "Castle," which the minority from the island in the North Atlantic generally found unamusing.[101]

After three years, Dr. Stolz and his family left Bethel Church that fall and were succeeded by the Reverend Edward Trevor, who could not have forseen the tempest which would lash him within the year. No one escaped the furious natural gales in the area, which observers called the most severe in years. Regarding another sort of danger, though, came reassurance in the Lighthouse Board's announcement that a first-class steam siren at Pilot Island Light Station would be sounded during thick weather in five second blasts at intervals of thirty-seven seconds.[102]

Just before Christmas, Henry Miner relinquished the postmaster's job (after eight years) to John Furlong although both Henry and Jesse went on carrying the winter mail on occasion. The office moved from Miner's cottage above the southeast shore of the Harbor to Furlong's dock on the west.[103]

1876

Washington Harbor's fisherman-farmer E.W. Steward might well have wondered later what perverse fortune led him to accept, early in 1876, the chore of sending news to the *Advocate*. The new scribe began harmlessly enough by asserting: "In this isolated spot little transpires of any interest to outsiders;" he next discussed a proposed tunnel connecting the Island with the mainland shore.

In mid-March, Steward reported that his neighbors were piling the piers with 3000 cords of wood to be shipped when the season opened. Coopers were busily preparing packages for the fishermen, some of whom had done well that winter despite the uncertain condition of the ice.

Then columnist Steward himself stepped onto the precarious ice of stating opinion in print. The missionary sent by the Bethel House of Chicago, he wrote, had not been a success as a converter of souls, and by his own conduct was setting a poor example. The writer suggested the pastor take passage on the first boat touching the Island, and concluded: "God will not be satisfied with pouring vials of wrath on the heads of such creatures, but will souse them with demijohns of vengeance." His descriptions of recent runaways by an ox team and a team of horses were mild by comparison.

In April, the scribe turned to seemingly non-controversial themes: seventy-six votes - the most ever - had been polled in the town election. Among the newly-elected town officers, correspondent Steward could list himself as a justice of the peace. On application of twenty-five freeholders, the column continued, the town had laid out a road from the southeast shore of Washington Harbor over Furlong's land to a point giving access from the south. Already a public dock was in progress which would facilitate shipment of timber and fish and the import of supplies which at the moment were scarce and high and none of the best. Island hens, "in this, our season of adversity," were shelling out fruit at a lively rate and their cackling furnished the pleasantest sort of music.

Meanwhile, the competing Sturgeon Bay paper had printed a defense of the embattled pastor, and the *Advocate's* editor arose to stand behind his Island correspondent. The latter, inspired by the onset of May, set aside distention to pen his longest and most poetic column to date.

"Spring gladdens the hearts of the inhabitants of this beautiful island," he began. The farmer has turned from his axe to the plow; the housewife is busy resurrecting her flowering bulbs. "Spring, Spring, beautiful Spring!" sang Steward. Fish were bringing $7.50 to $8.50 a barrel, a neighboring couple were blessed with a "beautiful rosy female infant," and four vessels had sailed from Detroit Harbor, "laden with nice, clean body maple, free from black knots and shakey butts."

The columnist was reporting a world essentially good, and late May inspired new rapture. Steward sang of "dewey sunrise...the beautiful, the tender, the sublime...the works of the Great Artist. ..." True, the new pier which he and his neighbors had built at Washington Harbor had been seriously damaged by the ice; but he found myriad attractions in the humble island life, and declared: "I would not exchange my cottage near the wood for all the marble palaces in Sturgeon Bay or Podunk."

Steward wrote his next *Advocate* column in the Door County jail. From this "dingy bastile" he stated the case for himself and six fellow prisoners: the new road and pier had impelled landowner John Furlong to file a complaint for trespass; the seven had been arrested on May 24 and, lacking bail of $500 each, lodged in the county lockup. "This comes very hard on us," mourned the prisoner, "two men being obliged to leave their sick wives, one with a babe just born, and the other about to be confined. Owing to the backward season, none of us got in our crops, and if we cannot get released … it will be very hard for us to provide for our families." [104]

The jailed seven, mostly farmers, were respectable citizens; John Larson was a town board member who would later become chairman, Steward was a justice of the peace. Town officers seem to have followed normal procedure in laying out the road, and in awarding Furlong $15 damages for crossing his land.

In a separate column, the editor pointed out Mr. Furlong's monopoly of the wood and fish business in Washington Harbor and its unfortunate effects on the Island's farmers and fishermen. The writer's sympathies favored the incarcerated seven, especially since the jail was built to house about half their number.

The Islanders were freed on the tenth of June, their case continued to a later date. By the twenty-second, the editor had "learned some particulars in regard to the trouble in Washington Harbor. …" The matter was somewhat different than he had been led to suppose, and Furlong appeared justified in his actions; the farmers might be well advised to let the matter rest for a while, and turn to improving their cut-over land. [105]

Considering Furlong's monoply of land and facilities in Washington Harbor and the increase in population and farming on the Island, clashes would seem inevitable. Probably both sides held sincere opinions - and both with some justice. Attacks on the powerful landowner (for example, in Holand's *Door County*, I: 293-95) should be weighed against the testimony of Mary Ellen Dowling and G. Ruby Cornell. Mary Ellen, a little girl in the 1870s, lived with her family on Furlong's land. She recalls his permitting Islanders to cut their winter's firewood on his property, to clear garden patches, pasture cows, pick berries, build and occupy dwellings on his holdings, all without charge. For some he built houses, charging very low rent (the Dowlings paid two dollars monthly). Some persons cut logs on his acreage without permission, but without consequences. In all, Miss Dowling remembered the Harbor's big landowners - Craw, Ranney and Furlong - as *"good dictators,"* who were *"good to the fishermen and everybody."*

We might also consider Mary Ellen's warm recollection of Mr. Furlong in light of the latter's aid to the Island's Roman Catholics. In a letter to Anne Whitney (February 23, 1951), Miss Dowling recalls: Father Hugenrath of Bailey's Harbor once stayed some two weeks in Furlong's house, held services there, on one day baptized 13 including 3 Dowlings - *"A big day for us."* The *Advocate* records that in June, 1877, when early settler James McDonald was *"nearing the end"* and needed a priest, Furlong got up steam in his tug and brought the Reverend Father Lagner [elsewhere Langner] from Escanaba to administer last rites.

The editor regretted, also, that a correspondent in Washington Harbor, "perhaps unintentionally," had done an injustice to the "Bethel missionary." The clergyman, he now understood, was a man of sterling qualities who had been greatly abused. "If the reverend gentleman feels aggrieved at any thing our correspondent has written, we humbly ask his pardon ... and by way of penance we are willing he should offer up prayers for our conversion until he is hoarse, and beg to assure him we need them muchly."

The Washington Harbor column a week later was signed only "S"; possibly Steward's last effort, it was more likely his successor's work. Many Islanders had turned out to hear visiting pastor Schultz of Indiana preach "an eloquent and inspiring sermon," closing with the earnest appeal, "Let brotherly love abound." The column reported "a fearful gale" of June 17 which seriously damaged the Island's fishing establishment, a visitation of Nature which prompted the anonymous "S" to admonish his readers: "The wind bloweth where it listeth, and they who sow the wind must reap the whirlwind. ..."

Perhaps cosmic balance demanded that the year's latter half should subside to a relatively placid close. Goodrich steamships glided into Washington Harbor on their trips to Green Bay; the Furlong trespass case was put off by the court into the future; in mid-August the *Advocate* announced "a new Washington Harbor correspondent. ... May he be heard long and often."

Washington Harbor.

To the Editor of the Advocate :
-In accordance with my promise, I write you a line or two from this extremity of the county.

-We had rather a tedious trip home in a fishing boat, having very light head wind and dead calms all the way, and accomplished the 55 miles in about 55 hours.

-It was surprising and gratifying to see the rapid growth of "garden sarse" and other vegetation in two weeks.

-We are getting quite a hot spell of weather.

-The natives are all grumbling and getting along.

Island town clerk and assessor Robert Severs made his newspaper debut with late-summer columns of peaceable news; "Garden sarse" had grown rapidly in the recent spell of hot weather; Andrew Koyen's store was enlarged and had a respectable stock of goods; Detroit

Harbor's District Number 2 was erecting a schoolhouse, with Dane H.O. Saabye the builder; no threshing machines nor reapers had reached the Island, but the hand-flailed grain from 100 acres had done well; the potato crop was promising and the "Colorado striped varmints" gave it little trouble.

Robert Severs may be one of the town's early residents most unjustly ignored in local history. Born in England in 1826, he came to America in '51 and to the islands in '52. He may have spent some years on St. Martin as did his brother Joseph; Robert first appears in the 1870 Town of Washington census as *"fisherman."* Elected town clerk in 1875, he was the incumbent at his death in 1901, having several times been assessor also. From December, 1877 to his death, he was Washington Harbor's postmaster. His columns appeared more or less regularly for a number of years in the *Door County Advocate*, and he was enumerator of several state and federal censuses. Described as a small, long-bearded man, *"proud as a peacock,"* who often

Potatoes and maple syrup were important cash crops

wore a swallow-tail coat, Severs was for the time and place a man of uncommon education and culture.[106]

The Reverend Father Garasche of Milwaukee visited the town and ministered to the needs of its Roman Catholics. The Reverend Captain Bundy of the Bethel Society's little schooner GLAD TIDINGS joined in marriage Andrew Johnson and Peter Hansen to the twodaughters of Anton Jacobsen, the last man fishing regularly from Rock Island. "The natives," columnist Severs summarized, "are all grumbling and getting along."

Perhaps town clerk-correspondent Severs was assessing conditions as accurately as more high-flown language could have done. There was little prospect that in the foreseeable future placidity would come to characterize the closely-circumscribed community which housed such a diversity of types and individualities wrestling, each very much in his own way, with a stubborn environment. But the violent winds of disparity and change which had buffeted the town's first generation were blowing themselves out; the softer zephyrs now moving bore gently if inexorably toward greater homogeneity and stability in the social structure.

The pressures which in the century's middle third had peopled the region mostly with eastern Americans had been largely replaced by a push from northern Europe. As time washed away the first generation of Island pioneers with their heavy dependence on the volatile fortunes of fishing, the community would gradnally root itself in a land-based life style of more conservative character, never free of its share of grumbling, but achieving more often than not its own workable method of getting along.

In October, with a tight presidential election expected, the *Advocate* printed the final evidence that the Town of Washington was regaining a state of normalcy:

81

Rock Island's lighthouse keeper William Betts, passing through the county seat, reported the Island "all right" for Republican candidates Hayes and Wheeler. Had they known at all of the island township in Lake Michigan, the Republicans might indeed have thought its politics were "all right." While losing the national popular vote by a quarter-million but squeaking into the White House with 185 electoral votes to 184, Hayes and Wheeler swept Town of Washington 47 to 18.

PART II
ICELANDIC SETTLERS

The section which follows is based upon and to some extent duplicates this writer's essay entitled "The Icelanders in Wisconsin" which appeared in the Wisconsin Magazine of History, *Vol. 56, No. 1 (Autumn, 1972), 2-20.*

"Icelanders practically monopolize Washington Island in the waters of Green Bay." This bit from a 1906 history of Wisconsin is but one example of the many misleading statements on the subject which have seen print in books, magazines and newspapers in the past century. We try here to present a reliable account of Washington Island's - and in passing, of Wisconsin's - part in the story of Icelandic immigration to the Western Hemisphere.[107]

The basic story is clear: in May of 1870 four young bachelors traveled from their native Iceland to Milwaukee. They worked thereabouts for some weeks, then sailed that autumn to Washington Island at the tip of Door County. That this minor movement should be worthy of notice one hundred years later is due to factors far more complex than has been generally recognized.

In the middle 1800s, Iceland shared with much of Europe those economic, social and political hardships which would force emigration to the New World. Together with a virtual Ice Age which had prevailed since about 1600, the ravages of sporadic volcanic eruptions made the environment so inhospitable that neither trees nor grain could be made to grow. Thus many Icelanders were not alone lured by the American promise of "free land, gold and green woods ..."; they were powerfully pushed by hunger and poverty to leave their homeland. Delayed it might be by Iceland's isolation, but mass emigration was inevitable. The only questions were When? and To what place?[108]

Eyrarbakki - the barren land Icelanders came from

    The very first - and very small - exodus in 1855 was a response to proselytizing in Denmark which the Mormon Church of Utah had begun as early as 1850. Because of widespread later acceptance of four emigrants to Wisconsin in 1870 as the trailbreakers of Icelandic immigration to America, this journey to the American West fifteen years earlier deserves mention, especially inasmuch as the Utah colony at Spanish Fork still exists today.[109]

    The established Icelandic church at the time was Lutheran. Hostility on the part of Lutherans toward a religion preaching polygamy, plus the fact that this migration found its driving force in Utah rather than Iceland, kept Icelanders from giving proper credit to the Spanish Fork colonists. They were followed to Utah in later years by other converts, but the early Icelandic Mormons' status as lost sheep probably denied them any chance to inspire a general migration to America.[110]

    Beginning in 1863 a limited number of Icelanders reached Brazil. Writers generally minimize or ignore this movement; and our inquiry to the Brazilian Geographic and Historical Institute drew the response that if Icelanders im-

**William Wickmann - the Danish businessman
who urged Icelanders to emigrate**

migrated to Brazil they were not numerous, and were
counted as Danes in the statistics. Thus we may reasonably
say that large-scale and important Icelandic emigration to
the Western Hemisphere was that which came to North
America. Despite the achievements of the Utah pioneers, it
was to other Icelanders that the opportunity fell to gain
lasting recognition for starting the westward flood. And
when those others left home, they were led by a lucky chain
of events directly into Wisconsin.[111]

By 1870, while a welcoming North American
continent still lay almost untouched by the hard-pressed
people of Iceland, 5212 Danes could already be counted in
Wisconsin - forty-nine of them on Washington Island. One
Dane, William Wickmann, who had worked for some years
in a mercantile house in Eyrarbakki on the south coast of
Iceland, came in April, 1865 to Milwaukee, where his sister
was the wife of the Danish consul. Wickmann found work

as a "German clerk," and corresponded with his former Icelandic employer Gudmundur Thorgrimsen, whom he later described as a father figure deeply respected and loved throughout a wide rural region. Thorgrimsen queried the Dane concerning possibilities for immigrants in America. Wickmann later wrote: "The good reports I could give about this country, soon brought the first Icelanders to Milwaukee. ..."[112]

Good reports indeed they were. Wickmann is said to have written that the waters of Lake Michigan were a bottomless mine of gold for the fisherman, and that Icelanders would have the same right as others to take out their share. It is reported that he also wrote: "Land can be had for homesteading and you can let your hogs run wild and catch them in the fall, fat." One can only guess how Wickmann would have described the bountiful fishing of thirty years earlier; by his day the U.S. Commission of Fish and Fisheries was reporting "an alarming diminution of the food-fishes of the lakes. ..." And while Wickmann and a few Icelanders eventually did well in procuring Washington Island homesteads, a good part of the Island's most desirable land was already in private hands by 1870.[113]

Critical factors at this point were the receptive attitude and the great influence of merchant Thorgrimsen in Eyrarbakki, who was called by one writer of his time "the only man in Iceland whose mind turned to America. ..." and who, two years later, was to permit his only son to join the westward-moving pilgrims. The establishment managed by Thorgrimsen was visited by residents of the entire countryside, and Wickmann's lavish praise of America reached a large and vitally interested audience.[114]

First to respond was one of the store's employees. Jon Gislason was twenty, son of a Lutheran minister, grandson of a superior judge; he had clerked in Thorgrimsen's store from the age of fourteen and is said to have cherished from an early age the longing to emigrate. He now owned an untouched inheritance from his father; America (and Wickmann in Milwaukee) beckoned; his employer gave his blessing. Gislason took the lead in planning the journey for spring, 1870. He was joined by twenty-four year old Arni Gudmundsson, a carpenter who had worked for Thorgrimsen, and by Jon Einarsson from Reykjavik, over twenty, who had "ridden" with a country doctor. Both men needed Gislason's financial help. Gudmundur Gudmundsson, nearing thirty, helmsman of a boat and considered to be a very lucky fisherman, paid his own way.[115]

Evidence leaves uncertain whether the four, or Wickmann, had made Washington Island their goal before they set out. But there can be no question whatever that, facing the entire New World, they were looking only toward Wisconsin.[116]

Their route was a tortuous one: from Eyrarbakki on the twelfth of May by road nearly fifty miles to Reykjavik. There they suffered the usual attempts to deter them. In America their letters would be censored though by whom, no one could say, as even the President could hardly be expected to read Icelandic. In the West, they might be scalped or eaten alive; escaping that, they might be taken into slavery. From Reykjavik the route led by post ship via the Faroe and Shetland Islands to Copenhagen; by steamship to Hull in England; by train to Liverpool; across a turbulent Atlantic to Quebec The Icelanders, braced between benches in steerage, played whist to pass the time. By eight days' halting train they traveled to Milwaukee, which they reached on June twenty-seventh. We find no evidence that they thought of their journey as "the beginning of Icelandic immigration proper" nor of themselves as "the fathers of the Icelandic immigration."

They had come to find a living, and Wickmann helped them get about it.[117]

"2 of them I got a place for on a farm near Milwaukee, and the other two by fisherman. When fall come, I brought them all up to Washington Island for to learn cutting timber. I had selected that place as headquater, and as most fit for them." All available evidence indicates that none of the four spoke English. Gudmundur Gudmundsson described them to his son years later as arriving "like cattle with tags on them." After the relatively rustic atmosphere of even their nation's capital (Reykjavik had some 2,000 inhabitants in 1870), Milwaukee County with nearly 90,000 must have seemed to the newcomers an overwhelming metropolis in which to make their way.[118]

More fit for them Washington Island probably was; but the popular concept of these "Vikings" settling comfortably into a familiar and welcoming environment which recalled their homeland is romantic fiction. The Island was prepared to assimilate the young Icelanders and to offer them hope for a future, but not without wrenching adjustments on their part which perhaps their youth alone made bearable. Only one had been a fisherman in Iceland where fishing differed greatly from Lake Michigan's. The first efforts by these emigrants from a nearly treeless land to earn a living on the forested island involved cutting trees with an axe. Moreover at least - in summer and winter - every endeavor demanded their endurance of a climate considerably more extreme than the one they had left.[119]

In no sense a raw frontier in 1870, the Island had been operating a town government for twenty years. It seems crucial to Wisconsin's future importance to Icelandic immigration that in their first year in the New World the newcomers were able not only to fit themselves acceptably into this established Island community, but to send favorable reports to the people back home concerning their life on Washington Island.[120]

Almost immediately, Wickmann and Gislason paid a Civil War veteran $400 for his wooded sixty-one acre homestead with 1500 feet of Detroit Harbor frontage. (Both newcomers gave their domicile as Milwaukee.) The purchase included some nets which enabled the Icelanders to catch all the fish they could eat.

When cash for other expenses was needed, Wickmann engaged an Irishman from the Island's northwest side to teach them the unaccustomed art of felling trees and cutting and splitting them into cordwood. Their misadventures in loading, unloading and reloading the first shipment onto a sailing scow and finally seeing her safely out of shallow Detroit Harbor for Milwaukee, amusing in retrospect, must have been at the time maddeningly laborious and frustrating. The vital facts in the Icelanders' building of this "nucleus of the first Icelandic settlement of the seventies" are that they survived, they persisted, and they gained a small measure of success.[121]

More than twenty years later, Wickmann recalled "The following spring (1871) I took more Icelanders to the Island, together with provisions, fishing nets, and other necessaries, and built house for headquater. They liked the Country very much, and soon Icelanders began to come to me in big loads." Here he summarizes and telescopes time drastically; but it is true that a few Icelanders reached Washington Island in 1871. Middle-aged Einar Bjarnason brought with him two children, leaving his wife and eight other offspring to follow two years later. This family left and returned to Washington Island, daughter Agusta married Jon Gislason, and some descendants retain connections with the Island for a full century. And Johannes Magnusson and wife arrived with their three year-old daughter. In their mid-forties, poor, with no language but Icelandic, the couple were looked upon by the firstcomers as unpromising material for the rigors of the new life. How they fared in the New World is told in an early letter to the homeland.[122]

While it is widely agreed that numerous letters were sent back to Iceland during the first few months, the first one now known about was written on March 8, 1872. In the same year a small section of it was printed - without the writer's name - in *Nordanfari* in the north coast town of Akureyri. Of the few possible authors, Jon Gislason or Gudmundur Gudmundsson seem likeliest. The letter is probably typical of many which fed the America fever in Iceland beginning in 1871.[123]

The weather has been rather good this winter, although it has sometimes been cold. ... I have been four days out on the ice and have caught fifty fish and sold them for about 7 dollars. People come here to buy fish and take it to different places and they pay 4 cents a pound. There are many fishermen here. They are leaving now as the ice is growing weaker. When no one comes to buy fish for several days, the fishermen leave their fish with each other and nobody ever steals one fish. ... Some get 30 fish a day, others none. "Changeable is the fishing."

Now let me tell the story of Johannes.

He came to us and started chopping wood. He did not do it too well at first, but as he was working with us he soon learned, His wife worked as housekeeper for her keep and that of the child. He stayed with us most of the winter. Then we put them into a house with an old widower who lives alone. They can stay in this house all summer for a low rent, as the man is going away to look for a job.

Johannes is supposed to sow the man's field, which is small. So his old woman can sow it, while he can seed and grub for others all spring for high wages. This winter he has chopped wood for 1 - 1 1/2 dollars a day, but used 30 cents for the three of them a day. He says he is not used to living on pancakes with syrup, pork and beans, fried pork and potatoes and white bread (wheat is the only grain they use for bread), and the 12-14 cups of coffee a day, because it is customary here to fill the cup as soon as it is empty during a meal and some people who are habitually thirsty can drink many cups of sweet coffee.

This is about the poorest food that one gets here, and Johannes says there is a great difference between that food and the one cup of milk in Iceland. Here some people eat five times a day. It is mainly Norwegians and Germans who eat so often. This food of Johannes' is bought at the hardest time here, so you see it is not very expensive to live here.

This place is one of the best for poor people to come to, for here they can live off the water and off the land. On the other hand it is one of the worst for people with enough money to go where the land is more fertile. I dare say there is no lazy and idle man in Iceland that I know, no matter how many children he has got, who cannot live a good life here. Even if the man would be too lazy to do anything, the wife would be able to grow enough in front of the house to live off, but I expect the man to fish in the lake, because there is quite enough fish close to shore, which is good for eating. The fish which is sold (whitefish and bleikja) has to be caught far from land.[124]

Contrary to popular belief, the Icelanders did not quickly nor ever "take over" the Island, small as it is. Neither were they unnoticed; and already the press was beginning to indulge in the exaggeration which was to persist for a century. The *Door County Advocate* of August 24, 1871, had quietly announced: "A number of Icelanders are expected at Washington Island this fall to make that place their future home. Quite a colony is expected." But on September 14, the same paper quoted the *Green Bay Advocate's* description of their coming as "an immigration unprecedented in the history of this country." Upwards of twenty families were said to have reached the Island, "accompanied by an agent, who speaks English, and who manages their affairs." (Beyond question the agent was Wickmann.) Grossly inflating the number on Washington Island, the article is nevertheless remarkable and tantalizing to the historian for the prescience shown in its final paragraph:

This is said to be the initial movement of a heavy immigration, numbering some 25,000 people, who are looking for new homes in this country. They expect to come to this region and to that bordering on...the Northern Pacific Railway and the Red River of the North. They are a hardy, industrious people...and we hear they are fully satisfied and even delighted with their first venture at Washington Island. ...

Parts of the item could well have come from a wishful and euphoric Wickmann himself; but in the light of the next seven years, developments - and the often disorganized trial-and-error manner of their unfolding - the references to the number of potential immigrants and to the eventual destinations in the Minnesota-North Dakota-Manitoba region seem almost clairvoyant.[125]

While Door County and the Green Bay region were thus early observing the newcomers, Wisconsin's official notice was slower. Annual reports of the Commissioner of Immigration of Wisconsin mentions no Icelanders until 1873, when fifty-nine appear as arrivals at Milwaukee between April and November - all listing Wisconsin as their final destination. 1875's report already showed a shifting pattern; 160 arrived at Milwaukee destined for other states, only three for Wisconsin.[126]

In 1872, the exodus gathered momentum, with emigrants from the north and south of Iceland totaling twenty, and called by a leading Icelandic historian "a promising group." The twelve men, three women and two little girls who sailed from Eyrarbakki in the south aiming for Milwaukee and Washington Island - the largest party yet to leave Iceland - were promising, indeed. One of them wrote from the Island over forty years later: "Several young men of this party were pretty well-educated, having frequented the Latin school of Reykjavik and one being a graduate ... Pall Thorlaksson." (When a seaman on the passage from Liverpool asked for recommendation as an emigrant guide, recalled Arni Gudmundsen, Pall wrote one - in English, Danish, German, French, Latin and Greek.) At least three others came from families which included judges or other functionaries. In the group also were merchant Thorgrimsen's nineteen-year old son Hans B.; Gudrun Ingvarsdottir, the betrothed of Gudmundur Gudmundsson of Washington Island; and the second Arni Gudmundsen to make the Island his home.[127]

From that summer of 1872 until autumn of 1875, Milwaukee was in effect the capital of Icelanders in America. Five of the southern party reached the Wisconsin metropolis by midsummer; the others remained in Muskegon, Michigan, hoping to replenish their dwindling cash by laying railroad tracks and stacking lumber. All postponed going on to Washington Island because of advice that no jobs were waiting there.[128]

Within weeks of the departure of the seventeen from southern Iceland, three young men sailed from Akureyri in the north with "only one thing in mind - to go to Washington Island and settle down." Warned by the Danish consul and others in Milwaukee that the Island had little to offer, they accepted city life, found jobs, and within weeks were writing letters home which could only excite fresh interest in emigration to America, if not to the Island.[129]

By September, several of that summer's immigrants to Milwaukee had banded together in what seems to have been the first Icelandic commune or cooperative in America. Leader was the brilliant Pall Thorlaksson, who had already written many letters to his father, Thorlakur Jonsson, in Iceland. The latter passed along the news to *Nordanfari's* editor, who published it in February, 1873. Pall had heard from the Icelanders on Washington Island. "They are contented there," Pall's father quoted, "but are finding the heavy forest on the Island hard to contend with." Pall felt the Island was not a good place for poor people to settle in, as it would take a good deal of money to clear the land to produce a good crop.[130]

Meanwhile, Arni Gudmundsen and thirteen others had reached the Island, and from "Washington Harbor" on August twenty-second, 1872 Arni wrote to his father in Iceland:

Concerning me and my companions: We were at a sawmill in Muskegan - from where I wrote you last - and since we were somewhat sick from the intolerable heat and the hard work, we decided to come on here to the island. ... We were there for three weeks. I earned 22 dollars, but all of that and more went for food and my travel expenses here. ...

Wickmann and Jon Gislason welcomed us kindly and we are all still here, though we have done very little the six days we have been here. I do piece-work for a Danish farmer in the next house, Koyen by name - he was a foreman on a farm in Jutland. I eat my noonday meal there, and breakfast and supper at Wickmann's. The job is to strip bark off cedar trees, which he then sells to the government to be used for telegraph poles. It's rather easy work - I get five cents for each one. ... If I worked the whole day I would get at least one dollar, in addition to board, which is good for a start. But I'm thinking of changing over to chopping down trees, for which I would get ten cents a tree. ... The boys - Hans, Bjarni and Stefan - have begun sawing and chopping firewood for Wickmann; that goes naturally slowly at first, and in fact they aren't being pushed.

Olafur Hannesson is in bed with a fever, but it is not considered serious. The other Olafur is both very sick and bored to death and wishes for nothing else than to come home again. ... If Olafur does not improve this winter, we will have to find some way to send him home in the spring.

...I myself like it very much on the island ... I have no homesickness, and my main thoughts are on earning money. This island is completely covered with a tall forest; it is not long ago that they started to settle here, so everything is still undeveloped. The houses are rather primitive, the roads poor, etc., but it's a good place to live, for there is plenty of work cutting down trees and fishing. I won't say that there is no better place for us here in Wisconsin, but it's no good to be constantly on the move - we can't afford that - so we will certainly spend the winter here.

In Chicago there is much murdering and stealing; not a day passes in which from one to four men are not murdered. This is hard on the police, but they can do little or nothing about it. It's good not to be there.
...It would make me happy to get a picture of the two of you. ...

   Your loving son,

   A. Gudmundsen

Six weeks later, on October 4, Arni wrote his mother:

We have been here on the island since I wrote last. I have been working for this man whom I mentioned in the letter to Father, and I have now moved there altogether. Things are going as well as they possibly could. I have not earned very much yet, but still more than my companions who have all been felling trees with Wickmann. I expect that I will be here this winter, no matter what the others do, because it is silly as can be to wander around from one place to another, even if one can somewhere find a better place than the one he has. But in the spring I will definitely go out into the world.
I have been feeling well ... and I have not strained myself working because I don't have any supervisor (whom they call "boss") to push me, and because my work is piece-work, which is nicer for everybody, especially those who have been "bosses" themselves, such as I was once considered to be. I have not been bored; it is all the same to me where I am in the world as long as I have something to eat and decent people to associate with - and they are as much here as in other places. One does not get drunk here every day, for little

alcohol is available, so this is the best place for men who want to stop drinking, or for those who don't want to pick up the habit - no loss in that, I say, and I'm sure you say so too.

Gudrun Ingvarsdottir looks after me, and she manages splendidly. My clothes are still in good shape, except for a hole in one of my yellow-brown socks. ... Socks like ours are not to be found in America. ...

I am sure that you would not miss Strokkholl if you had a house here on the island and enough coffee and salt meat soup, for it is very cozy here. Some of the boys are now thinking of getting some land in the spring, and I will most probably join them, but it will probably not be here on the island....

Olafur is still in bed with fever; I got him a place in the house where I live and he is well looked after. He lay for six weeks at the house of Gudmundur from Mundakot, but we thought the draft in that house was so great that it hurt his chances of recovery and so we took him away from there.

Now I have to tell you what we eat most of here: wheat-bread, butter, wheat-porridge, pancakes, coffee, potatoes, very little meat, an unceasing flow of syrup, cabbage, turnips, bacon, fish, and so forth. This food pleases me, and I have a ravenous appetite, but I still long for svid, hangikjot, meat soup, beef, lundabaggi, herring salad, kjammi, haddock, cod, lumpsucker, mallard, and lamb-steak ... I often dream of home and imagine that I have returned from America a big man - perhaps this will prove true some day, and then probably many things will be changed, things which would have best remained unchanged. ...

Your loving son,
A. Gudmundsen

Two days after Christmas Arni heard from home, and was warmed by the news of family and friends. On January 20, 1873, he responded:

... I have been in good health, still here in the same place chopping down cedar trees and making firewood, together with my three compatriots Bjarni, Stefan and Hans. Jon Gislason was also here, but he has given up farming for the time being. His friend Wickmann has left the island and gone to Milwaukee, where he is a clerk. It is safe to say that he (W) piled up nothing but debts here - he is not very thrifty.

The winter here began in the middle of November with snow and frost, and I don't remember it ever being as cold in Iceland as it was here around Christmas. It seems to me that the temperature was minus 25-30 degrees Reaumur - there are no thermometers around here. ... As of now there are at least two feet of snow covering the whole island. ... In spite of the cold we have never felt it working outdoors - more so in bed at night, because the house that we are living in really ought to be called a shed, like most of the houses on this island. No one remembers such a harsh winter as this and the last one. It is probably the large lakes lying all around here that make it so cold.

I don't feel like telling how much I earned this winter - it isn't much - but this much I can say, that I am not the worst worker among my compatriots here. Some of them are reluctant to go into the woods, but this is understandable for they are young and unaccustomed to hardship.

It's dull here on the island during the winter, since there is little or no communication with the mainland, except on occasion when someone walks to land, which is seldom because it's a long way over the ice. One amuses himself by making social calls, and people here are very hospitable. The people who live here get a newspaper which is published once a week by Scandinavians in Chicago and is called Scandinaven. *... Chicago is said to have been rebuilt for the most part after the terrible fire there last fall, and naturally more splendidly and elaborately than before.*

I suppose I will leave here in the spring. but I don't know where I will be going. It would probably be best to go to the western states, but it costs too much to get there. Most likely I will go to Milwaukee and work there this summer.

Just at this moment we have learned of the death of the daughter-in-law of the couple we are staying with, who recently moved from here with her husband into the house next door. She was in labor for almost a week without being able to deliver, and suffered horribly. it is terrible that there is no doctor in this out-of-the-way place, not even a reliable midwife, for it is probable that a good doctor could have helped in this case. This couple got married last year and lived happily together. You can understand what sorrow has come into this house today - to us Icelanders as well, for all we knew about the deceased was good. They had just decided to go to Denmark after a few years - they were not too pleased here.

Tell Mother that I am not really anxious for socks from her this summer, but I would prefer a couple of pairs of heavy mittens, best of all string knitted mittens - they hold up best in the woods. ... The two Olafurs are well again - they are working in Milwaukee.

I can assure you that I am still not sorry that I came here - in fact, I am glad that I took the initiative.... We expect that the mailman who carries out this letter will return with the letters from Home that arrived on the latest ship, and we look forward to them. ...

Are there perhaps many from Bakki coming here this spring? I have heard that Jon Palsson and Bjarni Siggeirsson, Bjorn i Gardbae and Jon the Strong are thinking of coming. I think it right for good workers to come who don't have good positions at home, especially if they know some English. But there is one disadvantage about this island, that there is little chance to practice English. There are mostly Danes and Norwegians here, though nine different nations are represented in this population of only around 300.

... Wishing you all a happy year and every blessing.

Your loving son,

A. Gudmundsen

P.S. ... I lost my glasses the other day in the forest - there are no glasses available here, so I can't do any reading. Now I am using Hans' glasses. but I can't see well with them. Your A.G.[131]

The first steamer touching the Island in spring of 1873 found several of the young Icelanders ready to jump aboard, and most of them never returned. By the end of August, Arni himself is found working in Milwaukee and living in the year-old cooperative household. Letters to his parents in summer and fall give many details concerning the new environment and the Icelanders' interaction with it. Of the summer's 150 new immigrants from Iceland, 100 stayed in Canada; 50 came to Milwaukee. They have found the heat tremendous at times. It is safe to counsel reliable girls to come here - all have found good places in the city, and ladies and gentlemen come every day asking for more. But almost half the Icelanders have only occasional jobs; and there are other problems:

I don't like it that they have started sending us paupers from Iceland now. One came here from Hrutafjordur, sent by the local authorities there, with his pregnant wife and three small children. He didn't have a penny when he got here, he is in bad health, is a poor worker, doesn't know the language - and yet these men are expected not only to survive but to get rich. And if things go wrong - which is not unlikely - these men say foul things about America. I really don't know what will happen to this fellow this winter, and to many like him. They managed to work enough to get through the summer, but in this city there is little or no work during the winter and these poor wretches can't go anyplace else. Well, it will all work out somehow.

When he wrote his parents in October, Arni could tell them how it was working out for the family he had described. A son was in the hospital, the father (Thordur Arnason) had died there, the Icelanders were scraping up ten dollars to bury him. At least one other Icelander would have to be fed by his countrymen, sent home at their expense, or put in a Milwaukee poorhouse - a painful choice.

The new surroundings clouded some bright events. A young Icelandic couple, Olafur and Gudrun, got married in September, with Arni a witness.

... We walked to the church, which is three English miles from here. Many Icelandic women were with us, and on the way their head-gear and costumes in general

were much laughed at especially by rowdies and other such rabble.

We came home from church in the trolley so we could avoid the bantering remarks of rowdies about the tasseled hats. That evening we had a party here, to which selected Icelanders were invited. We had plenty of beer and rum toddy, chocolate, coffee, pancakes and other baked goodies which are most common here.[132]

Concerning paupers from Iceland, Dr. Steingrimur Jonsson, in a November 2, 1972 letter to the writer from Reykjavik, stated that he and Dr. Finnbogi Gudmundsson of the Icelandic National Library agreed on this: Arni Gudmundsen's 1873 Milwaukee letters confuse two distinct families, and Thordur Arnason, father of C.H. Thordarson, in fact brought his family to America on his own resources. It still appears certain, however, that Arnason's family was left practically penniless when he fell sick soon after arrival and died after two months in a Milwaukee hospital.

Arni and many others are now thinking of leaving Milwaukee to seek jobs in Michigan and elsewhere. There have been good reports of Nebraska, where the land is excellent, and it seems likely that if Icelanders ever form a new colony, it should be there. A meeting of most of the Icelanders has just been held and a society formed which will raise funds to send searchers for a good spot for settlement. This will take time, perhaps two years.[133]

Meanwhile, the little colony which Arni had left was somewhat obscured in the forests of Washington Island. A correspondent of Milwaukee's *Journal of Commerce* visited the Island and wrote of "A Defunct Colony":

I was disappointed. I had expected to find upon the Island a colony of Icelanders. ... The colony, in fact, is much reduced and hardly affords a fair opportunity for studying the manners and customs of transplanted northmen. It consists now of just one Icelander who spends his time in fishing off Detroit Island, and whom I did not see. The settlement seems to have been only a temporary sort, consisting of people who stopped a while to get acclimated and get ahead a little by fishing and cutting wood, with the ultimate view of going to the cities or farms farther west. They have left a good reputation. They were so polite, the school master told me, that the other people used to laugh at them.[134]

Five weeks later, the *Door County Advocate* called the Milwaukee paper's item "a mistake, as all are there with the exception of two or three young men who are in Milwaukee temporarily. Thirty families more, of the same nationality, are on their way and will be there next week, to permanently settle on the Island." The future would show that the Island colony, small though it was, had set roots in the rocky twenty-odd square miles in Lake Michigan with what passes for permanence.[135]

Some of the more hard-pressed newcomers to Wisconsin (Thordur Arnason's widow and children among them) found temporary homes with Norwegian farmers, particularly in Dane County; others, with more resources, explored as far as Nebraska. And while it was still true in 1873 that Milwaukee was the focus of Icelanders arriving in the Western World, it is clear that in Wisconsin and even in the Old Country, many were already looking toward wider and hopefully richer fields elsewhere in the United States and Canada.[136]

On August 2, 1874, while celebrating in Milwaukee "the day of the settlement of Iceland one thousand years ago," and hearing, in a borrowed Norwegian church, the first Icelandic sermon in the United States, a group of forty-three Icelanders sent a petition to President Grant, asking that he send a man-of-war to Alaska that very summer, carrying three Icelanders who might assure themselves that Alaska looked promising for Icelandic settlement.[137]

The U.S. government began with splendid support, then lagged badly. Within a year, Canada was offering help to Icelanders interested in emigration, and a goodly share of the stream that flowed westward was eventually diverted to that country.[138]

Not all of Wisconsin's Icelanders believed their best hope lay in faraway places. In the same summer of 1874, Pall Thorlaksson explored northern Wisconsin and settled upon Shawano County, where he purchased considerable land. On his return to Concordia Seminary in St. Louis that fall, the young Icelander left his father Thorlakur Jonsson, his mother and several brothers and sisters among the new colony's handful.[139]

In letters to the editor of *Nordanfari* in Iceland, Jonsson listed the many advantages his countrymen would find in Wisconsin. And he pointed out Shawano's proximity to Washington Island, "where in all probability many of the Icelanders (at least those coming from fishing villages in Iceland) would settle, as fish is abundant in the lake and the island is said to be an ideal place for fishing stations." Within months, another Icelandic-American took issue; Sigfus Magnusson wrote *Nordanfari:* "I do not doubt that there is good fishing on W.I., but I do know that the gear used by the fishermen is very expensive, and that it would take the Icelanders many years to establish fishing stations there."[140]

According to the U.S. Commissioner of Fish and Fisheries *Report* for 1872 and 1873, p. 3, Lake

Michigan's Mackinaw boats averaged $100 in value, pound net boats $50, shanties $50, ice-houses $100. In 1885 the total investment in Washington Island's fisheries was reported as $7,980 and the products' value as $6,800; (*Report* for 1887, p. 138). These figures seem remarkably low. The *Door County Advocate* of July 31, 1873 reported "A good outfit consists of a boat and from forty to sixty nets, the whole worth perhaps from six to eight hundred dollars."

In 1875, with the Shawano colony swelled by new arrivals, Pall Thorlaksson founded there an Icelandic Lutheran congregation of thirty-five members, called by an Icelandic historian the first in America. And at a November meeting of the Icelandic Society in America (which had been founded in Milwaukee some two years before), Pall listed forty members in attendance - called by the same historian "the first Icelandic census taken in America. ..." On the list were the Arni Gudmundsen whose letters we have read, and also Johannes Magnusson, whose relish of Island food, described in the first known letter back to Iceland, had by now earned him the name "Johnny Pancake."[141]

The promising start in Shawano County failed to develop, and in 1879 the colony migrated bodily to Dakota Territory. With Milwaukee no longer pivotal in the general Icelandic immigration, there was left in Wisconsin only one actual Icelandic settlement - the small but persistent and always newsworthy colony on Washington Island.[142]

The progress of the little Island colony seems to have been steady, if slow. Perhaps because of its isolation, it was somewhat less disturbed by capricious comings and goings than were other settlements in Wisconsin and elsewhere. In general, the Island's Icelandic immigrants appear to have resigned themselves to its disadvantages and to have made use of its modest advantages.

The climate could sting them viciously; February, 1875 brought a temperature of minus 40 1/2 degrees. The soil was far from the nation's - or Wisconsin's - best. But the cordwood that could be harvested by miserably hard labor paid a great share of the farmer's annual store bill; and within reach were fish enough to put food on the family's table, and an occasional few dollars in its purse, and to give year-round livelihood to the commercial fisherman. And not only did time and the Icelanders' increasing familiarity with American language and customs erase their uneasy status as newcomers, but changes were occurring in the Island community itself which made their adjustment easier.[143]

Through 1874, Island government had remained largely in the hands of the New Yorkers and New Englanders who had built a community upon the Island's original wilderness. April, 1875 saw a town board of three Danes elected; all other officers were Norwegian or Danish save two, and Jon Gislason was made Highway Overseer in his district. The new town chairman was William Wickmann, the Icelanders' original sponsor, who was re-elected in 1876. While the easterners and a mixture of other stocks, including the Irish, were far from eclipsed in Island affairs, a Scandinavian flavor had begun to permeate the community. It seems likely that the very modest number of Icelanders who immigrated to Washington Island in the remaining years of the century found it less and less difficult to make themselves at home.[144]

Despite exaggerations often found in print, it is demonstrable that the number of Icelanders reaching the Island was modest indeed. Examination of the few authoritative sources and of local evidence indicates that the total number of adult male immigrants who settled permanently by the end of the century was close to twenty. Tallies frequently ignored women and children; including them might lift the Island's total of Iceland-born to a little over one hundred.[145]

While these limited numbers had a perceptible impact on their adopted island, their imprint on the imaginations of a few historians and many popular journalists was markedly deeper. The reasons for this phenomenon seem to lie outside the Island community and even outside the characteristics of Icelanders themselves, but rather within the preconceptions of the public at large. In 1875, for example, a steamer load of 300 Icelanders arrived in Winnepeg unnoticed while a local crowd searched the vessel for the expected stocky four foot tall Eskimo-like people with long raven hair.[146]

In 1898, a Wisconsin writer perhaps pinpointed the reason for the public's exotic mental image: "Few Americans have come in contact with any of this nationality. ... Iceland, the name, and the fact that the island reaches north to the Arctic Circle, at once suggests to our minds people living in small snow huts, clothing themselves in the skins of animals which they have killed and whose flesh they have eaten. ..." That the myths are widespread and persistent is indicated by a plaint in a modern travel folder from the Tourism Council of Iceland: "Contrary to belief that dies hard in some places, there are no Eskimos (or Polar bears) in Iceland." Local inquiry shows that such misconceptions have at least occasionally been expressed by visitors to Washington Island.[147]

While sentimental associations with the parent country and culture were undoubtedly maintained throughout long lifetimes by many immigrants to the Island, abundant published and unpublished evidence shows that Americanization began early for many of them and proceeded steadily. The complete absence of foreign-language schools was undoubtedly a factor, as were the absence of local or county Icelandic publications and the sporadic nature of even Danish church services. Most effective of all may have been the basic "Yankee" character of the political institutions the immigrants found on the Island.[148]

Perhaps we disposed too casually of foreign-language church services. As early as December, 1877, we find the Bethel trustees voting to have Sunday morning "preaching" in English and afternoon in Danish; this commenced at once. (*Centennial Echoes*, 27; *DCA,* January 31,1878.) In the *Advocate* of November 25, 1880, Robert Severs notes that pastor J.C. Peterson, recently from Denmark, "is supplying the pulpit of Bethel church. The service is Danish. A regular pastor is expected next spring."

In his September 3, 1885 column, Severs writes that Bethel church is to be painted and repaired, and the society will probably send a chaplain "so that we can have services in English once more." On October 28, 1886, another columnist reports Danish pastor L. Jensen leaving after two or three years as leader of the Scandinavian Lutheran congregation on the Island.

Summer of 1895 saw the Danish-Norwegian Baptist church reorganized into the Washington Island Baptist Church, according to recollections of the Reverend J.P. Thoms in the March 4, 1905 *Advocate.* The paper's Detroit Harbor column of March 14, 1896 reports that the Reverend N.P. Johnson fills the meeting house on Sunday evenings and has been urged to speak in the "Skandinavian" language on Sunday mornings.

An interesting twist appears in 1901; the February 16 *Advocate's* Detroit Harbor column describes the funeral of Dane Christian Neilson at which John H. Malloch conducted the services in Norwegian, and adds: "Mr. Malloch is an American and ... by self-study has acquired such a knowledge of the language as to speak it fluently."

At least a few of the community's leading Icelanders

The Arni Gudmundsen family

clearly worked hard to hasten their own integration. Jon Gislason spent several months at the University in Madison during 1876 and '77, partly to improve his command of English. Arni Gudmundsen became a naturalized American in 1882, by which time he had already entered town government as justice of the peace and had begun an incumbency of some thirty-five years as town treasurer. It is noticeable that while Irish voters still outnumbered Icelandic through 1878, the better-educated among the latter seem to have been the more likely to be entrusted with public office.[149]

Perhaps nothing the Icelanders did had more impact on the Island than did one accomplishment of Arni Gudmundsen's; he induced his younger brother Thordur to immigrate there in 1885 and set up the practice of

Gudmunder Gudmundsson   **Dr. Thordur Gudmundsen**

medicine. The emotional and sentimental effects on the isolated community of knowing for fifteen years as its only doctor a man born and largely trained in Iceland may have hastened the Icelanders' acceptance and probably fostered among outsiders the concept of the Island as an essentially Icelandic settlement.[150]

Concerning the Icelandic doctor, Severs announced in the September 3, 1885 *Advocate:* "We now have on the island a physician in the person of Dr. Gudmundsen, who is from Iceland and who is a brother of our town treasurer." The doctor had arrived, he said, just in time to set a broken arm and to attend a man who had cut off two toes with an axe. "There are several others who require a little 'coopering up,' and Dr. Gudmundsen is not likely to lack employment."

That exotic label on Washington Island may have gained currency, too, from Icelanders' writings. Early-comer Gudmundur Gudmundsson, for example, a working fisherman, became well-known for his articles and poetry printed in Winnipeg's Icelandic publications under the name Gamli Gvendur ("Old Gvendur" - a rather disrespectful nickname for Gudmundur). And Arni Gudmundsen's chronicles of the Icelanders' progress were widely published over a long period. His 1892 letter was used along with William Wickmann's by Harry K. White in writing "The Icelanders on Washington Island" for the Wisconsin Historical Collections; his description of the Island colony near the end of the century appeared in a well-known Winnipeg *Almanak*; forty-four years later the historian Thorsteinsson made use of Gudmundsen's *Almanak* account in his treatment of the Washington Island settlement; Hjalmar Holand, in his 1917 *History of Door County*, turned to "the Squire" for the Icelandic story; in 1930, Susan B. Davis drew heavily from Gudmundsen for her Island chapter in a young people's book.[151]

A more personal revelation of Gudmundsen's Americanization (and by inference that of his fellow immigrants) is a letter from Iceland to a daughter on Washington Island, on the occasion of his first visit to the land of his birth:

Reykjavik Oct. 22. 1919
Dear Lillie! - Rain nearly every day. ... Utmost tiresome weather. I have commenced to feel a little more at home ... but I am not in love with this place yet, the situation is

so different from what it is on the west side of the pond, that it takes time to get used to it. ...

(His sister has put up a bed for him in her house.) *She brings me coffee and cakes before I get up, - the old custom is in existence yet. ... What we eat? Generally some kind of sup for dinner and either fish or mutton potatoes & coffey, no bread. ... There are 37 boarders and they never ask for bread, I get bread however when I call for it, but am getting along pretty well with the Icelandic way of feeding yourself. ... Supper at 7, generally get Ragut or Plokkfisk* (ragout or hash of fish) *...- bread butter cheese of a very inferior quality, also blood sausag ... & tea. ... The price for the two meals have been kr100 per month - about to $25, and is on the raise all over, for everything in the way of eatables are very high.*

I and Thorgrimur had a pretty good time when we went to Eyrarbakka and I will have much to tell the former residents of that place, when I get home. ...

I have sometimes been thinking to start for home this coming winter ... (He thanks her for clippings sent to him; his brother-in-law "thought it grand to hear from the Island." He asks her to have the Door County newspaper sent to him in Iceland.) *I ought to be satisfied to spend a few months in the place where I was born. ...*

> *With much love to you all ...*
> *Your pater*
> *A. Gudmnndsen*

The expected boat came, but no letter for me. Have them write often. [152]

With all proper allowance for the changes of forty-six years, we cannot fail to notice that his word "home," (which in 1873 - and even in 1892 - referred to Iceland) now means a small island in Door County, Wisconsin. Perhaps better than the early settlers' replies to inquiring reporters in later years, this reveals Americanization of the immigrants' hearts and minds.

By 1970, the last weathered boards salvaged from an immigrant house the Icelanders built on Washington Island in the 1870s formed a part of the living-room decor in a modern seasonal dwelling. The name EYRARBAKKI was notably apparent and puzzling to many tourists only on the white steel sides of the ferry line's newest vessel. Perhaps the most evident trace of a living cultural heritage was a small herd of stocky Icelandic-breed horses grazing in Island fields. It should be noted that they were imported mostly by non-Icelanders.

In the Island's library, an oil painting depicts the ancient meeting place of Iceland's parliament. The inscription from the donor, Loftleidir Icelandic Airlines, reads:

**In commemoration of the
100th Anniversary of the
First Permanent Icelandic Settlement
in the United States Washington Island
1870 - 1970**

Gertrude Andersen - "Grandma Gertie"
first Icelandic child born here

On all the evidence, Washington Island's Icelandic heritage lies today largely in the realm of memory and sentiment, in a considerable body of published matter looking to a noteworthy past, and in the willing imaginations of hundreds of tourists who carry, on their visits to a small island in Lake Michigan, a mental image of exotic culture a thousand years old.

Bibliographic Notes

Considering that Washington Island is a small and remote bit of Wisconsin, it has received a surprising amount of notice in print. The number of books and articles, however, which contain fresh facts and interpretation are relatively few; the others form a chronological bucket brigade passing down through the years an often undistinguished brew of fact, misinformation and fiction. We deal here mostly with those reasonably available sources which treat largely or at substantial length with the islands in question.

Earliest (and found mostly in libraries) is Charles I. Martin's little *History of Door County* published in 1881 in Sturgeon Bay, where Martin edited the weekly *Expositor*. Besides offering the first full-length version we have found of the Death's Door legend - a version which seems to have strongly influenced later versions - Martin is valuable for some thirty short biographies of Islanders who arrived before 1871, for letters of recollections from three early Island residents, and for other useful facts.

Early Days on Washington Island, the only one of Jesse L. Miner's works available to the public, was originally a 72-page manuscript written about 1915, titled "History and anecdotes of Town of Washington and adjacent Islands by J L Miner." The version available today (originally published in 1937) follows the manuscript rather well, though with considerable modernization of spelling and punctuation and some emissions-. There is evidence that Miner may have owned Martin's *Door County*; but the former's writing is based firmly upon his own and his father's personal experiences. Unorganized though it is, the booklet should interest casual readers with its anecdotes and color; to the serious student of Island history able to compare it with other sources, *Early Days* is a valuable piece of work. (Concerning Miner's unpublished efforts, see *Rock Island*, 44-45, and footnote 38 of the volume at hand.)

The source most commonly drawn from in recent years by writers in all fields is Hjalmar R. Holand's two-volume *History of Door County,* published in 1917 in Chicago. His Death's Door legend, the model for most modern versions, is probably his greatest contribution to popular writers, but he devotes full chapters to Rock and Washington Islands. Despite some regrettable tendencies in Holand's writing of history (pointed out in Eric Wahlgren's *The Kensington Stone,* U. of W. Press, Madison, 1958, and on page 168, *Wisconsin Magazine of History,* Winter, 1967-1968), searchers for Island background in his *Door County* are perhaps served not too badly. We may find fault with his patently fictional Death's Door story and with his occasional looseness with names, doctoring of purportedly direct-quoted material, and tendency to permit others' contributions to pass as his own; but the general public may gain from his Island chapters a view of the island comrnunity's first forty years less misleading than is found in many newspaper and magazine features, thanks to Holand's avoiding the common "peaceful paradise" picture of the islands. Holand had access to Martin's *Door County* and apparently to Miner's three manuscripts when preparing his own *Door County* for publication.

No longer readily available, but of local value, is the fragile booklet published on the Island in 1933 by the Detroit Harbor Ladies' Aid Society. Such record-preserving efforts are of permanent value.

On a larger scale is *A Gleam Across the Wave* (available in a reprint) published in about 1949 by Arthur and Evelyn Knudsen. Basically a biography of lighthouse keeper Martin Knudsen, and valuable chiefly for his recollections of the islands from 1866 onward, the booklet recreates a pleasantly nostalgic atmosphere of earlier days.

Praiseworthy indeed is *Centennial Echoes,* published in 1965 by Bethel Community Church. Its compilation of a century of records and events plus its numerous excellent photographs should increase in value year after year.

An especially valuable source for the Island's post-Civil War generation is Anne T. Whitney's *Let's Talk About Washington Island,* first published in 1973 and re-issued in 1995.

To our notes on sources we must add one heavily drawn upon by those who followed him. The Reverend James Paul Thoms, a Chicago Baptist, began summering on the Island in 1895, owned a summer home before 1900, and from the first became active in the community's religious and intellectual life. Between October, 1904 and September, 1909, Thoms wrote for the *Door County Advocate* a series of articles on the features and history of Town of Washington; these demonstrably influenced G. Ruby Cornell, Anne T. Whitney, and Arthur and Evelyn Knudsen. Mary Ellen Dowling (see note 105) furnished Cornell and Whitney with facts from her own and her family's experiences, but also with some of Thoms' work from her "trunk" of newspaper clippings. (This bears on notes 44 and 64 in this volume.)

Through July, 1905, Thoms affected the pen-name "Semaj Luap Smoht," but dropped the disguise thereafter. He listed as his authorities "data of pioneer settlers," several standard histories and the *Wisconsin Historical Collections.* Some material first published by Charles I. Martin in 1880-81 is discernible, but it could have reached Thoms indirectly through the pioneers, as a handful of Islanders surviving in his day had local roots reaching back to the 1850s.

In reading his articles as history one, should be aware of a very considerable tendency to expand, embroider, dramatize and romanticize. Spelling of local family names is somewhat casual, and disturbing anachronism does appear. However, Thoms' observations of the islands in his own time are undeniably interesting and colorful, and he organized into palatable form a considerable body of formerly scattered facts and anecdotes.

One sheds a metaphorical tear for all the valuable bits of historical record which, down the years, have been fed to the stove or the bonfire or otherwise lost to posterity. Almost certainly such items would have greatly deepened and enriched our stores of knowledge today and for the future.

NOTES

1. R.G. Plumb, *History of the Navigation of the Great Lakes* (Washington, D.C., 1911), 80-83; James Strang, *Ancient and Modern Michilimackinac*, etc., (Beaver Island, 1854; reprint, Mackinac Island, 1959, George S. May, ed.), 23.

2. I. A. Lapham, *Wisconsin*, etc., (Milwaukee, 1846), 25.

3. Baraga to Leopoldine Foundation, June 3 and August 25. 1833; in Archives of Cause of Bishop Baraga. Marquette. Michigan.

4. Jesse Miner, *Early Days on Washington Island*, (Washington Island, 1937). 1 (hereafter cited as Miner, *Early Days*).

5. *Intelligencer*, May 30, 1835, January 8, 1834.

6. Details of the original light tower and dwelling are spelled out in contracts dated 1836 for building and fitting out the installation; these are in the National Archives, Washington. Some local sources (Jesse Miner, "His History of the Island of Potawatomie"; also a handwritten page of recollections by Jens Jacobsen, and reminiscences concerning light keeper William Betts' tenure, 1870-1886, both preserved by Anne Whitney) confirm the existence of a light tower and house different from the structure standing in the present century. A clue to the early tower's appearance might be the photograph of Bailey's Harbor Light shown opposite p, 256 in Hjalmar Holand, *History of Door County*, vol, I, Precise date of building of the present structure still eludes us; available evidence would place it between 1879 and 1886.

　　Further details concerning Potawatomie lighthouse appear in *Rock Island*.

7. Lot 5's 22.37 acres sold for $27.96, Ball's 110.36 acres for $137.95; Abstract of Sales of Public Lands, Door County courthouse. A good overview of Wisconsin land transactions is painted by Paul W Gates, "Frontier Land Business in Wisconsin," in Wisconsin Magazine of History, 52: 306-327 (Summer, 1969).

8. Letters from Commissioner, General Land Office to Fifth Auditor, Treasury Department and to Register & Receiver in Green Bay, January 2 to June 9, 1840; in National Archives. Suggestions that the beacon may have been intended for Bowyer's Bluff on Washington Island appear in Miner, "Pottawatomie" and on p. 169 of Michigan's Brief in the 1925 boundary dispute with Wisconsin.

9. Deeds, Door County courthouse. Lapham's *Wisconsin* had first been published in 1844.

10. *Green Bay Advocate*, September 21, 1848 (hereafter cited as *GBA*); p 166 of Michigan's Brief, in the action: *In the Supreme Court of the United States, October Term, 1925, Original No. 19 - In Equity* (hereafter *Michigan vs. Wisconsin*).

11. *Rock Island*, 15: Foster and Whitney, Report, etc., II: 395; *GBA*, May 10, 1849; *Review of the Fisheries of the Great Lakes in 1885* (GPO, Washington, 1890), 211.

12. Larry Gara, *Westernized Yankee: The Story of Cyrus Woodman* (Madison, 1956), 77, 95: deeds, and Abstract of Sales, Door County courthouse.

13. Miner, "Pottawatomie," *Early Days*, 2.

14. M.M. Quaife, *The Kingdom of Saint James* (New Haven, 1930), 94: *GBA*, January 31, 1850. Quaife gives the best of the many accounts of James Jesse Strang and his Beaver Island colony.

15. *GBA*, September 12, 1850: *History of the Great Lakes*, J.H. Beers & Co. (Chicago, 1899), I: 372: *Compilation of Public Documents*, etc., U.S. Light-house establishment (GPO, Washington, D.C., 1871), 532-537. R.S. Corwin, "Lake Michigan's Aids to Navigation," in *Year Book of the Public Museum of the City of Milwaukee, 1926*, 104, 109, calls Pilot's lighthouse the second on Lake Michigan; concerning a possible earlier light on Plum Island, see Eaton, *Death's Door*, 7, and Arthur and Evelyn Knudsen, *A Gleam Across the Wave* (Sturgeon Bay, c. 1949), 49. Anne Whitney's sources set the log schoolhouse in 1850, but this may be typical of several events which cannot be placed chronologically with absolute precision. 1850 census, Town of Washington, in State Historical Society of Wisconsin (hereafter cited as SHSW).

16. *GBA*, February 27, June 26, 1851. On May 14, 1851 Amos Saunders bought from Napoleon Stem and wife for $100 all but one acre of Government Lot 1, Section 25 on Washington Harbor (which Stem had entered at the Green Bay land office a year and a day earlier). In 1972 this 64 and 82/100 acres comprises all of Block 1, Haldor Gudmundsen Subdivision, plus the acreage eastward to Gasoline Town Road.

17. Photostats of 1851 proceedings against Mormons in U.S. District Court, Detroit; James Strang, *Michilimackinac*, 56-60; *Northern Islander* (Mormon newspaper published on Beaver Island), April 3, June 5, July 24, August 14, 1851 and July 15, 1852; GBA, May 29 through August 21, 1851.

18. James Strang, *Michilimackinac*, 66; Michigan Pioneer and Historical Collections, XXXII; 86; *Northern Islander*, September 9, 1852; GBA, May 20, 1852; Abstract of Sales.

19. Charles I. Martin, *History of Door County, Wisconsin* (Sturgeon Bay, 1881), 78; deeds, and Abstract of Sales; Miner, *Early Days*, 3, 5.

20. *GBA*, July 1 through August 12, 1852. In *Early Days*, 6-7.

21. *Northern Islander*, November 11 and 25, 1852; Miner, "Pottawatomie"; James Strang, *Michilimackinac*, 71; M. Cronyn and J. Kenny, *The Saga of Beaver Island* (Ann Arbor, 1958), 54-55; GBA, December 23, 1852.

22. *GBA*, January 27 and April 14, 1853, One emigrant guide among many: Daniel S. Curtis, *Western Portraiture, and Emigrant's Guide* (New York, 1852).

23. Deborah B. Martin, *History of Brown County* (Chicago, 1913), I; 257. Miner, *Early Days*, 3, 5, 14 sets the Negro colony in "*the early fifties.*"

24. Abstract of Sales; Miner, *Early Days*, 13, 2; C.I. Martin, *Door County*, 23; Julia Harrison Lobdell, *The Lobdell Genealogy* (Chicago, 1907), 164-166 (courtesy of Winona Young, Escanaba, Michigan); Ludlow P, Hill's narrative, in Michigan *Collections*, XXXII, 206ff; Wisconsin State Census, Town of Washington, 1855 (in SHSW); *GBA*, July 21, 1853. Records show a considerable diversity in the spelling of individuals' names. For example, in most courthouse records and in most newspaper mentions over many years, we find "*Lobdill*." In his case (and in several others) we attempt uniformity in the text, except where the material used forces a variation.

25. *GBA*, May 4, 1854; We often mention the Ranney brothers, leading Island citizens from the mid-1850s to the early'70s. Not surprisingly for that period their names appear in various spellings. The family name appears at least once as "Raney," and W.P.'s given name usually "Willet" but at least once as "Willett." Thanks to information given us on June 22, 1978 by Eugenie Betts VanTrees (Mrs. J.E.) of Memphis, we now understand that the Ranney usually listed as "Delbert" was properly "D. Elbert," often called "Bert." (Mrs. VanTrees' brother was named after this Ranney by her father, William C. Betts, a friend and employee of the Ranneys.) Subsequent to Mrs. VanTrees' help we found "D. Elbert" verified in one 1873 land transfer and on the 1870 census.

26. *GBA*, June 29, 1854.

27. *GBA*, August 17, 1854; *Wisconsin Historical Collections* (Madison, 1908), VIII ; 437; Holand, *Door County*, I; 279; personal communications, Mrs. Anna Einarson, Helen Anderson, February 1, 1972.

28. Miner., *Early Days*, 3 and "Pottawatomie"; an H.D. Miner letter in C.I. Martin's *Door County*, 22, says the church had meetings three or four years after Hamblin left.

29. *GBA*, October 5 through 26, 1854. New Yorker M.E. Lyman left the islands for the Door County mainland, became the first county judge and first county school superintendent; (Holand, *Door County*, I; 100, 111, 139-40; C.I. Martin, *Door County*, 78). Abstract of land sale. We are fortunate in being able to check Door County postal-history facts against the excellent unpublished work of James B. Hale, Madison.

30. *GBA*, June 22 through November 16, 1854. Strang's *Northern Islander*, November 2. 1854, claimed 2608 persons on Beaver.

31. This episode is based chiefly upon a long letter datelined *"Pottawatama (Washington,) Island, November 3d, 1855"* and signed *"J.E Wells."* The *Northern Islander's* editor, who printed it December 6, described it as *"in an unknown hand, having the appearance of gennine."* We are unable to identify J.E. Wells; but the circumstances almost demanded an assumed name. Although the letter has considerable flavor of authenticity, we must consider the possibility that the Mormon editor fabricated it.

32. *Northern Islander*, May 31, 1855; *GBA*, April 5, May 3, 1855; Wisconsin's Brief, *Michigan vs. Wisconsin*, 308.

33. 1855 Wisconsin Census, Town of Washington.

34. J.E. Wells' letter in *Northern Islander*.

35. J.E. Wells' letter; Miner, *Early Days*, 3; C.l. Martin, *Door County*, 79-80.

36. *GBA*, November 15, 1855; C.I. Martin, *Door County*, 22, 29.

37. Recollections in Miner, C.I. Martin and Holand place this fire from 1853 to 1862; but one can hardly question the *Green Bay Advocate* of February 21, 1856, which set it "*a few days since.*" Miner (*Early Days*, 2-3) has the boys frozen in 1853-54, but also links the time closely with Craw's fire.

38. Jesse Miner, unpublished manuscript, "Mail carrying Hotells and &c in the Pioneer days of the Peninsula and ajacent Islands," written about 1915; privately owned on Washington Island.

39. *GBA*, May 1, 1856.

40. *GBA*, May 22, 1856; Eaton, *The Naming*.

41. James Strang, *Michilimackinac*, 25, 87-88; for the Icelanders who *did* settle on Washington Island see Part II.

42. Miner, *Early Days*, 16, 1. The date of earliest application of the name *Dutch Town* to a small settlement on the Island's central north shore is uncertain. Reminiscing in later years, both Henry Miner and Jesse link the name with events of the middle fifties, in which period they were living there. The modern variant "Dutch Village" with tulip-windmill-wooden shoe connotations seems entirely misleading. Federal censuses of 1850, '60 and '70 list a total of 197 persons in German families against one lone Hollander in Town of Washington; and it is demonstrable that "Dutch" was current at the time to signify German.

43. *GBA*, June 26 through July 17, 1856; Wm. F. Lawler, "Michigan Islands," in *Michigan History* (1938), vol. 22, pp. 296-97; D.B. Martin, *Brown County*, 1 : 328-30; Cronyn and Kenny, *Beaver Island*, 56, 62-63; Quaife, *Saint James*, 171-79; C.I. Martin, *Door County*, 80. The basic facts of this episode are beyond question; some details, and most attribution of attitudes and emotions to the participants, are supplied here (as in some other places) by the writer.

44. *GBA*, June 18, October 22, 1857. Recollections of the hard winter are attributed by both Anne Whitney (unpublished typescript) and by G. Ruby Cornell ("Irish Had a Big Time," in *Door County Advocate*, September 20, 1940) to Goodlet Goodletson's speech at an 1866 picnic near the shore of Detroit Harbor.

45. C.l. Martin, *Door County*, 17, 37; Holand, *Door County*, I: 96-97, 115.

46. Wisconsin's Brief, 41, 308; Abstract of Sales, and deeds.

47. Miner, *Early Days*, 1, says 1856, but Door County marriage records make it 1859. Spelling of "Boice" from county records.

48. *GBA*, November 10, 1859. The pound net's date of entry into these waters and its rapid adoption are verified in *Review of the Fisheries of the Great Lakes* in 1885, compiled by Smith, Snell and Collins (Washington, 1890), 72.

49. *GBA*, January 5, 1860.

50. *GBA*, May 24, September 13, 1860; Miner, *Early Days*, 11; 1860 federal census, Town of Washington.

51. 1860 census; (German Andrew Irr was listed as French). Miner, "Pottawatomie."

52. Town of Washington records; Miner, *Early Days*, 12-14, "Pottawatomie."

53. *Door County Advocate*, March 22, 1862; Holand, *Door County*, I: 91. Henceforth, *Advocate* in the text signifies the Door County paper, cited in footnotes as *DCA*. Because of our frequent use of this newspaper from 1862 onward, we cite it only where it seems important. We gratefully acknowledge our debt, not only to this valuable institution, but to all those who have maintained and furthered it, and most especially to the present ownership and personnel, whose courtesies have far exceeded the usual limits of public service.

54. Miner, *Early Days*, 13, 19; *DCA*, March 12, 1863; 1860 census.

55. *DCA*, May 14, June 11, 1863. Save in describing environmental beauty, Rice's euphoric view of community lIfe hardly matches the record of the period. Concerning doctors, he must have considered only the big island; the *Advocate* of May 7, 1863 showed W. Ellis a newly-elected justice of the peace; on October 13, 1864 the paper had him on a draft list; a Rock Island tract was transferred late in 1868 for "*two hundred Dollars lawfull Money*" by a deed in which Ellis, wife Phebe, and the buyers are described as "*all resident of Rock Island*"; and Miner in "Pottawatomie" and "Mail" has Dr. William Ellis on Rock Island until 1869.

56. *DCA*, August 13, 1863. Miner ("Pottawatomie," *Early Days*, 13) says father John Beam was later killed in battle.

57. Deeds, Door County courthouse; *DCA*, November 26, 1863, March 3, 1864; Miner, *Early Days*, 13, 14, "Pottawatomie."

58. *Centennial Echoes* (Bethel Community Church: Washington Island, 1965), 22-23.

59. *DCA*, August 25, 1864 through March 30, 1865; Miner, "Mail." The Civil War service record of those (possibly fifty) veterans who lived (briefly or long term, pre- or post-war or both) in Town of Washington could bear extended study. Our research, hardly casual, leaves us unprepared to generalize. For what it may be worth, a Wisconsin Adjutant General's report in 1865 credits the Town with six "*Recruits*" and six "*Drafted*"; (Wisconsin's Brief, 309). However, there is abundant evidence that numerous men left the islands to enlist outside Wisconsin; for example, Henry Miner, who served with an Illinois regiment.

60. Deeds, Door County courthouse; *DCA*, August 3, 1865.

61. *DCA*, June 15, July 20, 1865. Mary Ellen Dowling tells the drowning story as received from her grandmother, Kathrine Weaver; she lists not a Frank Woolf but a Mr. Holly; (letter to Anne Whitney, March 19, probably 1950 or '51). Nolan's report was sent to the Green Bay paper, but reprinted in the *Door County Advocate* on July 20. The drowned fishermen are recalled in an Island column in the December 7, 1889 *DCA* as Love, Woolf and Weaver. The widow Weaver appears in the 1870 and '75 censuses as "Catherine," but her granddaughter's letter uses "Kathrine."

62. Miner, "Pottawatomie"; *Centennial Echoes*, 24, 32. H.D. Miner in C.I. Martin, *Door County*, 22 seems to imply that in about 1867 the church was instrumental in the town's outlawing of saloon licenses.

63. Miner in his "Mail" manuscript tells us: *"The only mail carrier drownded carrying the mail was Martin Oleson who was lost crossing the Door in the winter of 65 and 6 carrying his first & last mail. I think this the only mail Bag ever lost carrying the mail across the Door."*

64. See footnote 44. An 1866 picnic - a town-wide affair on July 15 celebrating the semi-centennial of the name *Washington* on the Island - was unreported in the paper (unless the school "*pic nic*" was it). This event is colorfully described both in G. Ruby Cornell, "Irish," in *DCA*, September 20, 1940", and in Knudsen, *Gleam*, 7-9. The first seems based largely upon recollections of Mary Ellen Dowling, whose relatives probably attended the affair; the second should embrace recollections of Martin Knudson who was twelve in 1866. Which writers learned what from whom remains unsettled; (see Bibliography).

65. Court records, Door County courthouse. Numerous interviews over some thirty years establish the existence of the local version.

66. Miner, "Mail." In recounting these pioneer trips with the mail Jesse generally gives his father (and sometimes himself) generous credit; considering the fearful difficulties and dangers (and the miserable recompense), no amount of credit would seem sufficient.

67. Abstract of Sales; C. Saabye's letter in Holand, *Door County*, I: 286-87; Mary Ellen Dowling to G. Ruby Cornell, February 14, 1940 (see Bibliography).

68. Town records.

69. Town records; Albert Goodmander, personal communication, 1961.

70. Miner, "Pottawatomie."

71. Miner, "Mail"; *DCA*, January 26, 1871; *Centennial Echoes*, 24, 32. Since December, 1865, Lathrop had owned 341 acres of the Island's south central area; (Abstract of Sales).

72. Town records.

73. *DCA*, March 3, 1870. The article was firmly based on writing done by Increase A. Lapham for Wisconsin's immigration efforts.

74. Winchell's notes are Wisconsin Exhibit 368 in *Michigan vs. Wisconsin*; they perhaps typify many questionable statements of fact and appraisals of Island life made by hasty visitors. We add a few points: Demos Soucie (variously spelled) is possibly the only avowed "Frenchman" to spend a considerable period of years in the town; (1870's census, though, shows him born in Maine). His 300 acres seem questionable; town records verify his owning eighty acres on today's Mountain Road in 1875. Soucie's figures on boats and fishermen also appear bloated; 1870 census lists 47 fishermen, not 300, implying possibly 16 boats, not 100. / Bethel church may have been used briefly as a school while the frame structure was a-building on the beach. / Peter McBride in 1870 was town treasurer and a town board supervisor; town records show that on November 1 he *"deeded town two acres for Cemetary for 50cts."* (Already there were numerous occupants; the deed said, *"on which 2 acres the Burying Ground is now occupied..."*) / At Jackson Harbor, Jesse Miner (*Early Days*, 13) has Civil War veteran

Edwin Richmond fishing in the early seventies; the 1870 census includes the Vermont-born fisherman, wife and child.

75. 1870 federal census, Town of Washington (SHSW). More details concerning Island agriculture around 1870 appear in *Rock Island*, 24, note 44.

76. Miner, "Pottawatomie"; deeds, Door County courthouse.

77. Eaton, *Rock Island*, 23-24. Washington Island's Andrew Irr, apparently fishing for a time at Beaver. Island, was involved.

78 Door. County deeds; Arthur Wickman interview, April 13, 1961. For details on Icelandic immigration see Part II.

79. Miner, "Mail;" We give a few *Door County Advocate* references to government contracts for carrying Island mail at this period: February 1, 1866; January 26, 1871; October 30, 1873; July 2 and November 5, 1874.

80. Town records; 1870 census

81. Town records.

82. *United States Commission of Fish and Fisheries: Report of the Commissioner for 1872 and 1873* (Washington, 1874). Part II; 3, 10, 72-74.

Four years earlier the schooner GRAPESHOT, wrecked on Plum Island, had also been a free lumber yard; (*DCA*, November 14, 1867 and Knudsen, *Gleam*, 13).

83. Town records; Isaac Stephenson, *Recollections of a Long Life: 1829-1915* (Chicago, 1915), 175.

84. *Centennial Echoes*, 32; *GBA*, September 7, 1871.

85. Town records. While Wisconsin made Republican C.C.Washburn governor with 53% of the vote, Town of Washington backed him 24 votes to 9.

86. Town records.

87. Early in the year (February 29 *Advocate*) the Ranneys had laid in a stock of ice and announced their intention of shipping fresh fish to Cleveland, which market had relied theretofore on Lake Superior for the unsalted product. We must question the reported 200,000 packages a year, in view of Ranney's reported 13,000 package estimate in another paper a year later. / In August the Ranneys had quit-claimed to the Reverend Peter Kitwood of Chicago (presumably in trust for Bethel Church as a parsonage location) 6 61/100 acres near Miner's post office on the Harbor's southeast side; (Door County deeds).

88. *Centennial Echoes*, 24; Town records. At least some of these roads had been planned in 1861, and apparently delayed by the War.

89. Town records. Town of Washington showed relative disenchantment with the Republican party. Whereas in 1868 it had supported U.S. Grant 48 to 3, and congressional aspirant Philetus Sawyer with 50 votes out of 50 cast, in 1872 it gave the same Republican incumbents a mere 23 to 8 advantage.

90. Arni Gudmundsen in Holand, *Door County*, 1: 291-293; and Arni's 1872-73 letters home to Iceland, see Part II.

91. 1870 census identifies Thomas McFadden as a laborer born in Maine. In *Rock Island* (p. 52) we mistakenly gave Jesse Miner smallpox in 1852; Mary Ellen Dowling (in Anne Whitney's papers) puts the pox in this later period. Knudsen, *Gleam* (27-28) gives interesting sidelights on this epidemic.

92. Arni Gudmundsen in Holand: I; 293: see also Part II.

93. Albert Goodmander suggests (February 12, 1972) that both his father, Gudmundur Gudmundsson, and Olafur Hannesson may have been fishing then from Detroit Island. Mrs. Gertie Andersen (August-September, 1967) makes it clear that her father, Olafur, fished from Detroit Island at least soon after this time.

94. Door County deeds. Perhaps the relatively good conditions among the fishermen impelled Islanders to support Republican governor C.C. Washburn 29 to 3, while Wisconsin turned him out of office 66,000 to 81,000 in the Democrats' only breach in the Republican monopoly between 1857 and 1890. (Town records; *Wisconsin Blue Book*, 1899: 374).

95. Deeds, Door County courthouse.

96. Town records; Johnson interview, February 11, 1971.

97. Miner, "Pottawatomie".

98. Town records.

99. Town records.

100. *Centennial Echoes*, 24, 26; *DCA,* July 8, 1875. For insight into the St. Martin's community see Margaret Coppess, *Island Story: The History of Michigan's St. Martin Island* (1981).

101. Like several structures (and events) in the town's history, this building eludes documentation by this writer as to precise date; interviews with Islanders who lived there (e.g.: Mrs. Gertie Andersen, Mac Magnusson) place it very close to this year.

102. *Centennial Echoes*, 24, 26.

103. James B. Hale, postal data; Miner, "Mail." On the Wisconsin scene the Republicans eased their candidate into the governor's mansion by an 85 to 84 ratio. In Town of Washington they could breathe more easily; Republican Ludington got 21 votes to the Democrat's 11. (*Wisconsin Blue Book*, 1899: 374; Town records.)

104. *DCA*; Town records; town census of 1870 and 1875.

105. Holand, *Door County*, I, 293-95. Dowling's letters to Anne Whitney (November 26, 1951 and others undated); Dowling to G. Ruby Cornell (February 14, 1940).

106. C.I. Martin, *Door County*, 23-24; Town records and Town censuses; *DCA*; interview with Albert Goodmander, February 27, 1968.)

107. Reuben Gold Thwaites et al., *Wisconsin in Three Centuries*, 5 vols. (New York, 1906), III: 56.

108. Arni Gudmundsen quoted in *Door County Advocate*, March 23, 1889; Thorsteinn Th. Thorsteinsson, *Saga Islendinga i Vesturheimi* (History of the Icelanders in the Western World), 5 vols. (Reykjavik and Winnipeg, 1940-53), II: ix, 111 hereafter cited as Thorsteinsson, *Saga*). [This work, of which volume II was supplied to the writer by Professor H. Bessason of the

University of Manitoba, is described as definitive from the Icelandic viewpoint by Dr. Richard Beck, past president of the Icelandic National League of America (to writer, December 22, 1969) and by Dr. Finnbogi Gudmundsson, Chief Librarian of Iceland's national library (to writer, June 15, 1965). Relevant parts of volume II were translated for the writer by Miss Alfheidur Einarsdottir of Reykjavik.] *Hornafjordur and Southeast Iceland* (tourist folder published c. 1967, Reykjavik, by Icelandair); Thorstina Walters, *Modern Sagas* (Fargo, N.D., 1953), 210; Robert E. Delaney, "A Visit to Washington Island," in *American-Scandinavian Review*, LI: 165 (June, 1963); William Wickmann to Harry K. White (no date), and Arni Gudmundsen to Harry K, White, October 19, 1892, (both in Division of Archives and Manuscripts, State Historical Society of Wisconsin); *Encyclopedia Britannica*, XII; 46 (Chicago, 1963).

109. *Green Bay Advocate*, January 31, 1850, September 7, 1854; Walters, *Modern Sagas*, 33; Valdimar Bjornson, "America in the Making," p. 6-7 (WCAL radio broadcasts of October 14 and 21, 1948) ; mimeographed. At this same time, King James Jesse Strang's Beaver Island Mormons were making wide-ranging efforts to gain converts for their colony. We cannot resist speculation as to the possible outcome had the Beaver Islanders and not Brigham Young's Utah Mormons converted these early Icelanders. In that case the earliest Icelandic colony in the Western Hemisphere would have been located on a Lake Michigan island some seventy miles northeast of Washington, but would almost certainly have been irretrievably scattered at Strang's death in 1856.

110. Val. Bjornson, "America," 7; Thorsteinsson, *Saga*, 3. As cited in Harry K. White, "The Icelanders on Washington Island," in *Wisconsin Historical Collections*, XIV: 340, Jon Bjarnason, Bishop of the Icelandic Lutheran Church in Canada, took notice of Icelandic colonies as distant as Brazil, but ignored Utah completely.

111. Thorsteinsson, *Saga*, 67-107; Brazilian Institute's First Secretary to writer, April 20, 1964; Knut Gjerset, *History of Iceland* (New York, 1924), 459; Agnes Rothery, *Iceland*, New World Outpost (New York 1948), 188; *Encyclopedia Canadiana* (1958), V: 227; Val. Bjornson, "America," 7.

112. Theodore C. Blegen, "The Competition of the Northwestern States for Immigrants," in *Wisconsin Magazine of History*, III: 25 (September, 1919); 1870 manuscript census of Town of Washington, in Archives Manuscripts, State Historical Society of Wisconsin; *Door County Advocate*, December 29, 1870; William Wickmann to Harry K. White. The latter based his "Icelanders" article chiefly on Wickmann's letter, which internal and external evidence places (probably early) in the period May 3, 1892 to 1898./ Personal communication of Wickmann's son Arthur (1961) credits the father with speaking and writing five languages.

113. O.S. Thorgeirsson, *Almanak/1900* (Winnipeg, 1899); Olof Sigurdson, "Icelandic Settlements in Manitoba," etc., (M.A. thesis, University of Manitoba, 1929), 36; Thorsteinsson, *Saga*, 111-12; *Milwaukee Journal*, July 21, 1932; U.S.Commission of Fish and Fisheries, *Report* for 1872-

1873 (Washington, 1874), 14-15; Abstract of Sales of Public Lands, Door County courthouse.

114. Thorsteinsson, *Saga*, 112, 121-22.

115. *Ibid.*, 112-13. One cannot ignore the suggestion in several places [e.g., "The 'Little Iceland' in Northern Lake Michigan," in *Literary Digest*, September 9, 1922, 45-48; Albert O. Barton, "The Scandinavian Element in Wisconsin," in Milo M. Quaife, ed., *Wisconsin, Its History and Its People* (Chicago, 1924), 123; Fred L. Holmes, *Old World Wisconsin* (Eau Claire, 1944), 220] that Gudmundur Gudmundsson (and possibly some of the others) reached Milwaukee in 1869. Thls aberration appears traceable to a *Milwaukee Journal* article of August 27, 1922, itself well sprinkled with demonstrable inaccuracies wholly unsupported by any primary source except an interview with Gudmundur Gudmundsson (aged eighty-two) and neighbors. In personal communication, February 12, 1971, Albert Goodmander (son of Gudmundur Gudmundsson) denied any possibility that his father might have come to America otherwise than with the three mentioned companlons in 1870.

116. Walters, *Modern Sagas*, 33; Thorsteinsson, *Saga*, 114; Gudmundur Gudmundsson in F.L. Holmes, *Old World Wisconsin*, 220-21; Arni Gudmundsen in Hjalmar Holand, *History of Door County*, 2 vols. (Chicago, 1917), I: 291; Arni Gudmundsen to Harry K. White; William Wickmann to Harry K. White; Arthur Wickman, personal communication, April 13, 1961; Sigurdson, thesis, 36.

117. Thorsteinsson, *Saga*, 113; Delaney, "A Visit," 164; Rasmus B. Anderson, "Icelandic Immigration," in *Chicago Record-Herald*, August 21, 1901; Arni Gudmundsen to Harry K. White.

118. William Wickmann to Harry K. White; Albert Goodmander, personal communication, February 27, 1968; C. W. Paijkull, *En Sommer l Island* (Copenhagen, 1867), 11; *Wisconsin Blue Book*, 1899, 686-87.

119. Lawrence Gislason, personal communication, June 28, 1965; Thorsteinsson, *Saga*. 112, 114; Icelandair leaflet, "The Weather in Iceland," (probably Reykjavik, 2nd edition, 1967).

120. Miner, *Early Days*, 2; Town of Washington records, 1868-1881; census, Town of Washington, 1850, 1860, 1870; Delaney, "A Visit," 164.

121. Deeds, Door County courthouse; Thorsteinsson, *Saga*, 114, 116; William Wickmann to Harry K. White; Arthur Wickman, April 13, 1961; Lawrence Gislason, June 28, 1965.

122. Wickmann to Harry K. White; Thorsteinsson, *Saga*, 118; Albert Goodmander, February 12, 1971; Arni Gudmundsen in Holand, *Door County*, I: 292.

123. Thorsteinsson, *Saga*, 118-19. The periodical *Nordanfari* was published for a number of years in the chief town of northern Iceland; in the 1870s its editor opened his columns generously to the earliest emigrants and their followers. In *The Icelandic Canadian*, Vol. XXX, No. 4 (Summer, 1972), page 37, Valdimar Bjornson credits Gudmundur Gudmundsson with the letter; Thorsteinsson's *Saga* suggests the same possibility, but says: "It can not be proved. ..."

124. We follow three slightly varying translations of the first letter; Alfheidur Einarsdottir after Thorsteinsson, *Saga*, 118-20; Angantyr Arnason, "Icelandic Settlements in America," (M. A. thesis, University of Manitoba, 1929), 6-7; Professor H. Bessason.

125. Estimates of numbers of emigrants from Iceland to North America vary in the half-dozen most trustworthy sources from 16,000 to 30,000; a preponderant number finally settled in the general region the Wisconsin papers mention. Walters, *Modern Sagas*, v, 31-32; Kirk Munroe, "Some Americans from Oversea," in *Harper's*, (February, 1898), 437-40.

126. Annual reports of Commissioner (1871-1875) and Board (1881-1886) of Immigration of the State of Wisconsin.

127. Thorsteinsson, *Saga*, 120-25; Walters, *Modern Sagas*, 34-36; Arni Gudmundsen in Holand, *Door County*, I: 292, We must identify two Island Arni's: the 1870 Arni Gudmundsson (known later as "Little Arni" and as "Arnl G. Le Grove" and variants) spent most of the ensuing sixty years on the Island as farmer and carpenter; the 1872 Arni Gudmundsen (quoted above from Holand) lived most of the next sixty-five years there, reached some local eminence, and was published widely on the subject of the Island's Icelandic immigration. / Only the brilliantly talented Thorlaksson never tried wresting a living from the Island; he and his cousin Hans B. Thorgrimsen (who left the Island after one winter's try at "farming" under Wickmann's tntelage) later became clergymen, and *"the leaders of their countrymen in both spiritual and secular rnatters,"* (Walters, *Modern Sagas*, 39-41, 57-65, 83-85, 88-93.) In a slight discrepancy between Thorsteinsson and Walters as to whether one adult or three in the party were women, we follow the former, corroborated by Arni Gudmundsen.

128. Thorstelnsson, *Saga*, 231; Arni Gndmundsen, Muskegon, Michigan, July 31, 1872 to his parents in Iceland. This and five other letters sent from Washington Island and Milwaukee in 1872-73 were acqnired thus: On the writer's 1968 visit to Iceland an interview with daily newspaper *Morgunbladid* was arranged by Dr. Steingrimur Jonsson and Dr. Finnbogi Gudmundsson. Our appeal in the paper for unpublished early letters from Wisconsin eventually brought word of copies of Arni's letters which his parents had sent in the 1870s to their daughter in the north of Iceland. Through the efforts of Dr. Gudmnndsson the letters were Englished by Professor Robert Geiger Cook, at the time Fulbright Professor at the University of Iceland, and sent to Washington Island. Thus the letters were returned to the region in which they had been written nearly a century earlier.

129. Thorsteinsson, *Saga*, 130. The Milwaukee letters of Jon Halldorsson (August 21 and September 8, 1872) and of Johannes Arngrimsson (September 22, 1872) appeared in *Nordanfari* January 31, 1873; they encouraged many who were considering emigration to Milwaukee - now the *"focal point of the steadily increasing Icelandic immigration to the United States."* (Walters, *Modern Sagas*, 45.)

130. Val. Bjornson, "America," 9; Johannes Arngrimsson, September 22, 1872; Thorsteinsson, *Saga*, 126-31; Thorlakur Jonsson, February 3, 1873.

(Valdimar Bjornson of Minnesota was the featured speaker at Washington Island's centennial celebration banquet on July 8, 1970. / Thorlakur Jonsson's letters and parts of Jon Halldorsson's and Sigfus Magnusson's were translated for us by Mrs. Hrund Skulason, University of Manitoba.)

131. Arni Gudmundsen to parents, August 22 and October 5, 1872, and January 20, 1873. Concerning the speaking of English on the Island Arni betrays a parochial viewpoint reflecting his location on the Island's south side, where Scandinavians were prominent. Eight years later a post office with the Danish name "Fagerwick" would open on Detroit Harbor a few hundred feet from Wickmann's - and Arni Gudmundsen's - 1872 location. Actually, of the Island's 385 population in 1870, the families of native-born family heads totaled 150; adding Irish,Scottish, English and Canadian natives, the English-speaking might have totaled two-thirds, Scandinavians and others one-third. / Fred Koyen told us (February 28, 1972) that the young woman tragically lost in childbirth must have been the first wife of his uncle Fred; and the Danish farmer from Jutland in whose house Arni Gudmundsen lived was Edward William Koyen, father of the bereaved Fred.

132. Arni Gndmundsen in Holand, *Door County*, I: 291-93; Arni Gudmundsen to parents, August 31 and October 5, 1873. Among the offspring left destitute by the unfortunate Thordur Arnason was six-year-old Hjortur (later known as Chester H.) Thordarson, who, as a celebrated electrical inventor and manufacturer, would eventually receive high honors from Iceland and the honorary M.A. from the University of Wisconsin. After Chester's death in 1945 the Wisconsin Conservation Commission paid $175,000 for his Rock Island estate, and the University of Wisconsin bought his rare book collection for $300,000. Thorsteinsson, *Saga*, 172-73; Steingrimur Jonsson, "Islenzkur Uppfinninga Madur i Bandarikjunum," in *Lesbok Morgunbladsins* (Reykjavik. May 7 and 14, 1967) ; Ralph Hagedorn, "Bibliotheca Thordarsoniana: The Sequel." in *Papers* of the Bibliographical Society of America, vol. 44 (1st quarter, 1950); *U. of W. Library News* (Madison, March, 1966), XI No. 3: 1; Eaton, *Rock Island* (Washington Island, 1969), 27-43, 47-50; Neil M. Clark, "The Flare of the Northern Lights Started Thordarson On His Quest," in *American Magazine* (December, 1926), 37.

133. Arni Gudmundsen to parents, October 4, 1873. The society seems to be the "Icelandic Association of the Western World" mentioned in Walters, *Modern Sagas*, 45-46. Arni Gudmundsen kept a notebook listing Washington Island's members of this group in 1874 (19 members), and in 1875 (17), and the Island's Icelandic non-members (24 including several children). Notebook privately owned on Washington Island; lists translated and interpreted by Dr. Finnhogi Gudmundsson, Reykjavik.

134. Reprinted in *Door County Advocate*, July 31, 1873.

135. *Door County Advocate*, September 4, 1873. Most evidence, including Gudmundsen's notebook, shows that the number of families given in newspapers in this instance and some others is greatly exaggerated.

136. Val. Bjornson, "America," 8; Sigurdson, thesis, 38; Thorsteinsson, *Saga*, 215-17.

137. Walters, *Modern Sagas*, 46, 205, 209-10. Thirty-six of the signers list Milwaukee as their residence; five give Washington Island; one, Waterford, Wisconsin; one, Leland, Michigan. However, six "Bjarnasens" seem to belong to the Einar Bjarnason family, some of whom came to Washington Island in 1871 and were later to re-establish themselves there.

138. Walters. *Modern Sagas*, 211-15, 228-29, 49-58; Thorsteinsson, *Saga*, 221-22, 239-50. Walters' research in the National Archives illuminates this abortive movement germinated in Milwaukee beyond anything we have found elsewhere.

139. Thorsteinsson, *Saga*, 226.

140. Thorlakur Jonsson to *Nordanfari*, January, 1875; Sigfus Magnusson, (probably from Wisconsin), July, 1875, to *Nordanfari* (printed October 26).

The present writer, following various sources including translations from the Icelandic, may have corrupted the name of the periodical, which usually appears as *Nordanfari*, not *Nordurfari.*

141. Thorsteinsson, *Saga*, 227-29; Walters, *Modern Sagas*, 83-84.

142. Walters, *Modern Sagas*, 62-63; Thorsteinsson, *Saga*, 230; Clark, "Thordarson," 183-84.

143. *Door County Advocate*, February 18, 1875; Lawrence Gislason, June 28, 1965; journals and ledgers of Corrigan's (later Gislason's) Store, 1882-1899 (Island Archives); Arni Gudmundsen to Harry K. White; William Wickmann to Harry K. White.

144. *Door County Advocate*, April 29, 1875 and April 20, 1876; Town of Washington censuses, 1870, 1880. As late as 1899, the *Wisconsin Blue Book* (p. 394) showed Door County with 66.8% of its voters foreign-born.

145. Thorsteinsson, *Saga*, 115-16. Arni Gudmundsen's listings: of Icelandic Immigrants; of marriages he performed, 1881-1900; of Washington Island Militia members, c. 1905; (all privately owned on Washington Island). O.S. Thorgeirsson, *Almanak*, (Winnipeg, 1900) ; Corrigan's and Gislason's ledgers, 1880-1901; Town of Washington census, 1895; Arni Gudmundsen to Harry K White; William Wickmann to Harry K. White; Arni Gudmundsen in Holand, *Door County*, I: 291-93; poll list, 1881, in Town of Washington records; Albert Goodmander, June 8, 1972.

146. Walters, *Modern Sagas*, 55.

147. Harry K. White, "The Icelanders," 335-40; Loftleidir airlines folder, *Iceland Welcomes You* (probably Reykjavik, c. 1968) ; Mrs. Oddur Magnusson, personal communication, 1941.

148. William Wickmann to Harry K. White; *Door County Advocate*, 1870-1889; Town of Washington records.

149. Holand, *Door County*, II: 240-41, 386-87; Town of Washington records; *Door County Advocate*, April 23, 1937; copy of Arni Gudmundsen's naturalization certificate.

150. William Snow Miller, "Dr. Thordur Gudmundsen: The Icelandic Doctor of Washington Island," in *Wisconsin Medical Journal*, vol. 38 (May, 1939), 404-08; notebook of Dr. Thordur Gudmundsen, privately owned on Washington Island; Thorsteinsson, *Saga*, 116. In Arni Gudmundsen's bringing Thordur to the Island we are reminded of young Arni's outcry in 1873 ; *"It is terrible that there is no doctor... ."*

151. Arni Gudmundsen to Harry K. White; Thorsteinsson, *Saga,* 111-17; Holand, *Door County,* I: 291-93; Susan B. Davis, *Wisconsin Lore for Boys and Girls* (Menasha, 1931), 222-37.

152. Arni Gudmundsen, Reykjavik, to Lara (Lillie) Gudmundsen Hagen, October 22, 1919.

INDEX

Gislason, 66, 71, 88, 91, 92, 97, 100, 108, 111, 131, 134
GLAD TIDINGS, 81
Goodletson (also Goodlet), 71, 125
Graham, 18, 28, 34, 62
Grover, 47, 61
Gudmundsen, 9, 95, 96, 98, 99, 102, 104, 107, 111, 112, 113, 123, 128, 129, 131, 132, 133, 134, 135

H

Hamblin, 30, 124
Hannesson, 97, 129
Harris, 44, 46

I

Icelanders, 5, 6, 64, 66, 67, 68, 73, 74, 83, 85, 86, 87, 88, 89, 90, 91, 94, 95, 96, 101, 102, 103, 104, 105, 106, 108, 109, 111, 112, 113, 115, 125, 129, 130, 134
Indians, 7, 14, 15
Ingvarsdottir, 95, 99
Irishmen, 58, 60
Irr, 61, 64, 125

J

Jacobsen, 81, 122

K

KITTY GAYLORD, 62
Kitwood, 45, 47, 49, 50, 128
Koyen, 79, 97, 133

L

Larson, 26, 65, 77
Lathrop, 56, 58, 60, 64, 127
Lobdill (also Lobdell), 28, 32, 33, 35, 36, 39, 41, 49, 61, 124
Love, 45, 47, 126
Lovejoy, 36
Lyman, 30, 124

M

Magnusson, 91, 106, 107, 129, 133, 134
McBride, 58, 59, 65, 127
McDonald, 39, 41, 52, 53, 54, 62, 63, 78
McFadden, 45, 67, 129
McGill, 28, 40
MICHIGAN, 18,29
Miner, 9, 14, 17, 19, 20, 21, 25, 27, 34, 36, 52, 53, 58, 62, 64, 65, 66, 67, 71, 74, 118, 119, 122, 123, 124, 125, 126, 127, 128, 129, 131
Mormons, 20, 23, 31, 32, 33, 35, 36, 37, 86, 123, 130
MORTON, 26

N

Nolan, 34, 35, 38, 39, 40, 45, 47, 50, 126
Nordanfari, 92, 96, 106, 131, 132, 134
Norwegians, 5, 24, 40, 54, 58, 60, 93, 102

O

O'Neill, 62, 71
Ottosen, 55

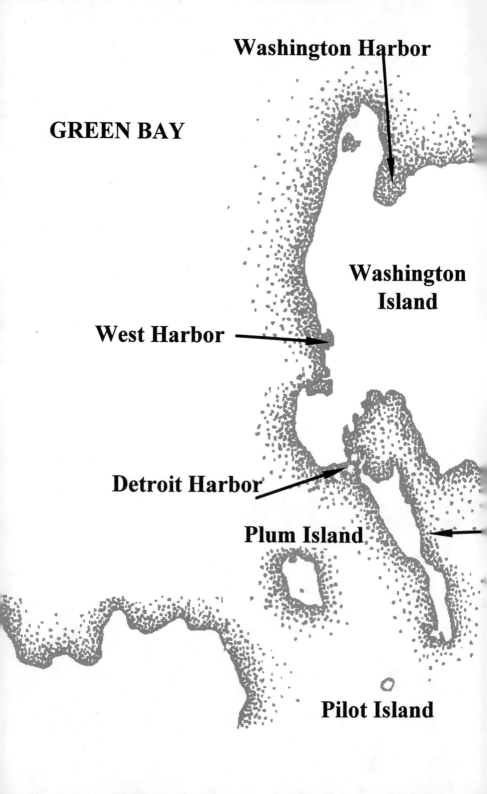